I0423389

Editor-in-Chief and Founder:
    Lyndon H. LaRouche, Jr.
Editorial Board: *Lyndon H. LaRouche, Jr. , Helga Zepp-LaRouche, Robert Ingraham, Tony Papert, Gerald Rose, Dennis Small, Jeffrey Steinberg, William Wertz*
Co-Editors: *Robert Ingraham, Tony Papert*
Managing Editor: *Nancy Spannaus*
Technology: *Marsha Freeman*
Books: *Katherine Notley*
Ebooks: *Richard Burden*
Graphics: *Alan Yue*
Photos: *Stuart Lewis*
Circulation Manager: *Stanley Ezrol*

INTELLIGENCE DIRECTORS
Counterintelligence: *Jeffrey Steinberg, Michele Steinberg*
Economics: *John Hoefle, Marcia Merry Baker, Paul Gallagher*
History: *Anton Chaitkin*
Ibero-America: *Dennis Small*
Russia and Eastern Europe: *Rachel Douglas*
United States: *Debra Freeman*

INTERNATIONAL BUREAUS
Bogotá: *Miriam Redondo*
Berlin: *Rainer Apel*
Copenhagen: *Tom Gillesberg*
Houston: *Harley Schlanger*
Lima: *Sara Madueño*
Melbourne: *Robert Barwick*
Mexico City: *Gerardo Castilleja Chávez*
New Delhi: *Ramtanu Maitra*
Paris: *Christine Bierre*
Stockholm: *Ulf Sandmark*
United Nations, N.Y.C.: *Leni Rubinstein*
Washington, D.C.: *William Jones*
Wiesbaden: *Göran Haglund*

ON THE WEB
e-mail: eirns@larouchepub.com
www.larouchepub.com
www.executiveintelligencereview.com
www.larouchepub.com/eiw
Webmaster: *John Sigerson*
Assistant Webmaster: *George Hollis*
Editor, Arabic-language edition: *Hussein Askary*

EIR (ISSN 0273-6314) *is published weekly (50 issues), by EIR News Service, Inc., P.O. Box 17390, Washington, D.C. 20041-0390. (703) 777-9451*

European Headquarters: E.I.R. GmbH, Postfach Bahnstrasse 9a, D-65205, Wiesbaden, Germany
Tel: 49-611-73650
Homepage: http://www.eirna.com
e-mail: eirna@eirna.com
Director: Georg Neudecker

Montreal, Canada: 514-461-1557

Denmark: EIR - Danmark, Sankt Knuds Vej 11, basement left, DK-1903 Frederiksberg, Denmark. Tel.: +45 35 43 60 40, Fax: +45 35 43 87 57. e-mail: eirdk@hotmail.com.

Mexico City: EIR, Sor Juana Inés de la Cruz 242-2 Col. Agricultura C.P. 11360 Delegación M. Hidalgo, México D.F. Tel. (5525) 5318-2301 eirmexico@gmail.com

Canada Post Publication Sales Agreement #40683579

Postmaster: Send all address changes to *EIR*, P.O. Box 17390, Washington, D.C. 20041-0390.

Signed articles in *EIR* represent the views of the authors, and not necessarily those of the Editorial Board.

Building a World Land-Bridge: Realizing Mankind's True Humanity

The Uniqueness of the Human Mind

April 7—Today's Schiller Institute Conference in New York City, "Building a World Land-Bridge—Realizing Mankind's True Humanity," marked a success for Lyndon LaRouche's idea. Although further and fuller reports follow, with more to come in our next issue, that much can already be said with certainty.

Helga Zepp-LaRouche opened the conference with a comprehensive and inspiring address, "Beyond Geopolitics and Polarity: A Future for the Human Species." She laid bare the immediate threat of annihilating war, and showed that the idea of the World Land-Bridge, which she developed with her husband from 1989, provides the only durable guarantee for peace. She outlined a dialog of civilizations in which each of the world's civilizations is represented by the cultural highpoints of its history, such as Germany's Weimar Classic, and the United States as it was first conceived by Benjamin Franklin and Alexander Hamilton.

Helga was followed by former U.S. Attorney General (1966-67) Ramsey Clark, who wove his own long experience into an account of recent world history which underlined the alternative to the war policies of most of the post-Kennedy U.S. Administrations.

The next speaker was a truly unique figure from China, that nation's leading professor of journalism and the leader of much else as well, Li Xiguang. Professor Li has led a decades-long pilgrimage on behalf of the Silk Road,—across Central Asia, and down each of the three North-South routes, and back again. He has led no fewer than 500 of his students on this pilgrimage with him since 1990, and has written two volumes on the New Silk Road. Although his goals for the Silk Road are not religious goals—they are the same as ours—Professor Li models himself on the great Chinese cultural heroes, the Buddhist monks Xuanzang (602-664) and Faxian (337-422). Both made long and arduous trips along the Silk Road, and brought back the first real knowledge of much of world civilization to China, including Sanskrit language and culture and Buddhist scriptures in the original.

Xuanzang spent no less than 16 years on this voyage, and returned with 600 Indian texts. In 646, at the Tang Emperor's request, he completed his 12-volume work, "Great Tang Records on the Western Regions," now one of the primary sources for the study of medieval Central Asia and India, and the basis for the Sixteenth Century novel *Journey to the West*, one of the Four Great Classical Chinese Novels.

The afternoon session, "The New Scientific Frontiers," highlighted the space program. LaRouche PAC leader Kesha Rogers opened it with a vivid presentation. The climax of that session was a question-and-answer period with Lyndon LaRouche by Skype. He led most of the questions back to the cardinal issue that changes in the physical system, and in the future of mankind, are created by the thinking human mind itself; no animal can do this. Mankind is organized by his own acts of this type; it is these which lead either to failure or to success. This is the mind of the true scientist, of which Einstein is an example. But this account is only a characterization; his actual answers should be studied in detail.

The climactic third panel, the musical and cultural panel, began in the evening. To do it justice, rather than trying to cover it below, it will be a major feature of the next issue of *EIR*.

Attendance exceeded 230, not including the core membership. About a dozen foreign countries were represented, whether through diplomats, cultural associations or in other ways. Many musicians attended, and at least five people from the Brooklyn church where we performed the Messiah during Easter. This may have been our largest conference ever.

In conclusion: This conference was a victory for an idea of Lyndon LaRouche, that of the Manhattan Project which he unveiled in October 2014. Yet at that time, as Einstein wrote of Kepler, he was "supported by no one and understood by very few." Lyndon LaRouche, the inventor of the Strategic Defense Initiative, and later the inventor, with his wife, of the Eurasian Land-Bridge, had once more invented a new and wholly different original idea. Again it has proven true.

EIR Contents

www.larouchepub.com Volume 43, Number 16, April 15, 2016

CC A-SA 3.0 /Alancrh

Cover This Week

A Chinese high-speed train developed by CSR Corporation, the CRH380A, is designed to operate at a cruise speed of 217 mph.

I. New Silk Road Becomes the World Land-Bridge

Building a World Land-Bridge— Realizing Mankind's True Humanity

NEW YORK, April 7—The Schiller Institute conference today in New York City, "Building a World Land-Bridge—Realizing Mankind's True Humanity," began with Helga Zepp-LaRouche's keynote on this theme. She was introduced by conference moderator Dennis Speed. The edited transcript follows.

Dennis Speed: On behalf of the Schiller Institute, I want to welcome everybody here today. I will begin with a greeting to the conference from the Chinese Chamber of Commerce of New York. It reads:

Dear friends,

On behalf of everyone at the Chinese Chamber of Commerce, I extend a warm greeting to all in attendance at the Schiller Institute conference. I truly believe the scientific triumphs of the past century, and the advancements in technology, were not through sheer luck or chance. Rather, I believe it is the collective efforts of our species as a whole that allow us to grow and prosper beyond what we could ever accomplish as individuals. Only through cooperation between all nations can we *all* achieve a greater goal. The conference of *The New Silk Road Becomes the World Land-Bridge* will discuss issues including the designs for the development of Southwest Asia, as well as a path for United States recovery. We sincerely wish the conference will be very successful, and the attendees have a wonderful stay in New York City.

Sincerely,
Justin Yue
Chairman of the Chinese Chamber of Commerce in New York City.

You know, New York City was founded by Alexander Hamilton and George Washington. I am not talking about the chronological founding, but the fact that as an American city, it was founded on the principle of a single unified government. Hamilton's role with George Washington in the first American Presidency, was a revolutionary one, which was more important than the victories on the battlefields of Trenton, Saratoga, and Yorktown. Hamilton's four documents on the National Bank, the constitutionality of the National Bank, the nature of credit, and the nature of manufactures are the basis for the real United States. It is that real United States that the Schiller Institute seeks to place back on the world stage in collaboration with, particularly, the nations of Brazil, Russia, India, China, and South Africa, in the pursuit of the policy called the World Land-Bridge.

The danger of warfare which now lurks and pulsates from a collapsed trans-Atlantic system is what brings us here today, in part. The Schiller Institute has been doing conferences in Egypt, and has spoken at conferences in Russia and India and many other locations in the past weeks. And in that light, and in that context, I'd like to introduce the person who has campaigned tirelessly for the World Land-Bridge policy.

The first glimmer came in 1989, when she and her husband, Lyndon LaRouche, first enunciated this policy as the Eurasian Land-Bridge, shortly after the fall of the Berlin Wall. In 1996, in June, a conference was held in Beijing, which put the idea of the New Silk Road on the map, and at that conference, the founder of our organization spoke, and that conference basically precipitated what then became known as the Shanghai Cooperation Organization. Many other developments followed. And now, on this stage, we are at the point where, if our keynote speaker is listened to, there's a world that can be made, can be created, of cooperation, and not destruction.

Stuart Lewis/EIRNS

Helga Zepp-LaRouche, shown here addressing the April 7, 2016 Schiller Institute Conference in New York City, warned that we are closer to World War III than we were at the height of the 1962 Cuban Missile Crisis, and emphasized the only way out is world-wide development based on the principle of the Chinese New Silk Road policy becoming the World Land-Bridge.

It's always an honor and pleasure to introduce the chairman and founder of the Schiller Institute, Helga Zepp-LaRouche.

Helga Zepp-LaRouche: Dear guests and friends of the Schiller Institute, this conference is taking place at a very serious moment, and it has no lesser goal than that which has been defined by my husband Lyndon La-Rouche with the Manhattan Project: that we have to turn the United States back to its founding principles. We have to get the United States away from its present imperial orientation and the idea that it must pursue a unipolar world, and turn it back to the identity of a republic, as the Founding Fathers and the Constitution designed it.

This goal is something which almost the whole world thinks is impossible. I can assure you that, outside of the United States, the thinking people think the United States is hopeless, and I can assure you that that is a very common feeling. Many people don't travel to the United States any more because they think it has

become a place of horror. Yet, achieving this goal, to turn the United States back into a republic, is going to determine, in all likelihood, the fate of the entire human species.

There is right now an absolutely eerie tension in the air, because many people who don't always say it, know that we are right now closer to World War III than even at the height of the Cuban Missile Crisis. It has been stated by military analysts and nevertheless, there is no peace movement. There is nobody in the street talking about the fact that we are close to World War III. In the 1980s you had hundreds of thousands of people marching in the streets of Germany against the SS-60 and the Pershing 2. Today the situation is more dangerous, and experts have explained that if there were an incident, the warning time to launch general thermonuclear war would be three to six minutes.

Only a few people are saying that, while the vast majority of citizens in the United States and Europe is marching like lemmings towards the cliff.

I want to highlight a case of a 78-year-old pensioner, a retired teacher from the German city of Kaiserslautern, who, two days ago, had his suit rejected at the third level of the federal administrative court in Leipzig, where he tried for the third time to sue the German government for allowing the United States to use the air base at Ramstein for a relay system for drones, without which the drones could not be sent to the Middle East and elsewhere. [He said] that this was against the German Constitution, which does not allow Germany to ever again launch a war of aggression, or help other countries to do so. The judges ruled again that matters of international law can only be taken up by states, and not by individuals, but this pensioner, 78 years old, is planning to take this issue to the highest constitutional court, in Karlsruhe.

One is almost reminded of the story in the Old Testament in which God was about to punish the cities of Sodom and Gomorrah for their sinful behavior, and was then persuaded that if there were at least ten righteous men there, the punishment would not be carried out. And I must ask: Are there ten honest men to stand up today?

The Strategic Picture

Before I come to the solution, how we can get out of this crisis, let me review the very dire strategic situation. We are now having 12 days of joint military drills involving the United States and the Philippines, Australia, and Japan. The exercise is called Shoulder to Shoulder, and for the first time ever, the U.S. Secretary of Defense, Ashton Carter, will go there to be on site next week. Now yesterday, Carter said that the enemies of the United States are first, Russia; second, China; third, Iran; fourth, North Korea; and fifth—oh yes, there was terrorism.

In parallel, you have the largest ever U.S.-South Korean military exercises until late April, also involving many troops. The Philippine exercise includes an amphibious landing to simulate taking one of the disputed islands in the South China Sea. The Philippine military is also sending a U.S. high-mobility artillery rocket system designed to shoot down aircraft. It is the first time that these exercises have included Australia and Japan, in the effort to build a quadrilateral military counter-alliance to China.

Secretary of Defense Ashton Carter appeared at the Center for Strategic and International Studies April 5, saying that Russia and China are the primary enemies of the United States.

Now other things are taking place in the region. Two weeks ago, the Philippines allowed the United States to have access to five of its bases near the disputed waters in the South China Sea, and they renewed the Enhanced Defense Cooperation Agreement. Now this is against the Philippine constitution, but they bypassed it by allowing the U.S. troops within Philippine bases, so that the Constitution would not apply. Now also Japan has a new national security law which went into effect last Tuesday; the national Diet passed a new security bill breaking away from the pacifist Constitution of Japan, in order to enhance the alliance with the United States, and with it, the power to exercise the right of collective self-defense.

Now, the whole world is watching: Does this mean that Japan is going to go back to its militarist past?

There is a tendency in Japan right now, to move into alliances with other claimants of the contested territories [in the South China Sea] to contain Beijing.

Now where is all of this leading? China's position concerning these waters is written in what it calls the Nine Dash Line in the South China Sea, and China claims that these are territories which historically have belonged to China, including the right to reclaim land and build bases on the Spratly Islands. China also says—and it is true—that this does not represent a violation of the freedom of the seas. It will only improve the living conditions of the people there and improve protection against pirates, without hindering the passage of other ships.

Now the Philippines in 2013 filed a case in the International Court in the Hague, insisting on its right to exploit the South China Sea waters in its 100-nautical-mile exclusive economic zone, as defined in the UN Convention on the Law of the Sea. China did not accept to be a party to this case—which is its perfect right—but is questioning the legitimacy of the case. The court should have at that point dismissed the case, but it accepted it, and the ruling is expected at the end of April or beginning of May. The Chinese Defense Ministry said that it has the absolute right to then declare an Air Defense Identification Zone (ADIZ).

Now at the Nuclear Security Summit in Washington, which has just taken place, President Xi, in a discussion with President Obama, told Obama that China would not accept any behavior in the guise of freedom of navigation that violates its sovereignty in this region. One day later—exactly one day later—the United States announced a new patrol near the disputed islands in the South China Sea, and U.S. Navy officials announced that they plan to conduct more and increasingly complex exercises in the future. So the United States is playing a chicken game against China, increasing the tension over violations of opposite claims, in anticipation of the Hague ruling, to create an atmosphere in which, they hope, China would not dare to set up an ADIZ.

But China has already said that it will defend its rights in the South China Sea. So the question is, could there be a war between the United States and China over some relatively worthless rocks and reefs in the ocean? Could it be that the United States will go to a war with China on the Philippines' behalf?

Obviously the South China Sea is of geographical significance for China, but the interest of the United States is geopolitical, and it uses the same reasoning as in the Trans-Pacific Partnership (TPP) to affirm its right to set the rules in Asia. The United States insists that it will defend a unipolar world, that it is the only super-power, and that it will not allow any other nation to meddle in that status. Obama's claim that Russia is only a regional power is absurd, given that Russia has a nu-clear arsenal which is a complete strategic match to that of the United States. And Putin has just executed very brilliantly a military flank in Syria against ISIS, demon-strating that Russia is absolutely needed if you want to have political solutions. Russia played a positive role in the P5+1 negotiations with Iran, and is now making possible the end of the war in Syria and helping to end that war. There are many leaders in the world who have said that, without Russia, you cannot solve existential problems such as terrorism, ISIS, and the refugee crisis in Europe.

Imperial Intention Contested

One should recall that these territorial disputes in the South China Sea are the result of the imperial inten-tion dating back to the Versailles Treaty and the Paris Peace Conference in the aftermath of World War I in 1919, whereby the former German colonies in the Pa-cific Islands north and south of the Equator were given in part to Japan, which at that time caused a tremen-dous sense of injustice in China, leading to the May Fourth Movement. All the people in China thought the Versailles Treaty was a complete fraud. And as we know from European history, it laid the seeds for World War II.

The same game was repeated at the San Francisco Peace Conference after World War II, where John Foster Dulles arranged for China to be excluded, de-spite the fact that China had the highest casualty rate in Asia against the Japanese, and fought the longest. But the Western powers drew the map in Eastern Asia with-out China, and John Foster Dulles deliberately de-clared certain Asian frontier territories to be without owners, an old imperial trick to manipulate future con-flicts, as was the case with the Sykes-Picot Agreement for Southwest Asia and the 1919 Trianon Treaty for the Balkans.

British system/Wall Street operative John Foster Dulles played a leading role creating the conditions for the South China Sea Conflict at the April-June 1945 formation of the UN at the San Francisco Peace Conference, by excluding China from participation. Here, Dulles (standing second from the right) witnesses the Japanese signing of a security treaty with the United States, Sept. 8, 1951, by then Prime Minister Yoshida Shigeru.

The fact is that the unipolar world has already ceased to exist. It is a fact that China is rising; the United States is losing its hegemony. China is already exporting many more technologies than the United States. It is educat-ing far more scientists and engineers, and the word in the science community internationally is, if you want to get anything done in frontier science, the place to go is China.

So China, except for a couple of minor corrections in its stock market, is doing very, very well economi-cally. Do not believe what the *New York Times* is trying to tell you every day. Because China has embarked on the policy of the New Silk Road and the Maritime Silk Road—the One Belt, One Road policy—for huge proj-ects to connect all of the countries of Eurasia through infrastructure development and high technology in-vestments. It is so attractive that 60 nations are already cooperating with China. It has created, together with other BRICS countries, a complete, alternative economic system that includes the Asian Infrastructure Investment Bank (AIIB), which has immediately had 60 founding members, despite the United States bringing enormous pressure on everyone not to join it; the New Development Bank, which is now already operating; the New Silk Road Fund and Maritime Silk Road Fund; and many other such institutions. There is a tremendous attractiveness of this program for a New Silk Road in the spirit of the ancient Silk Road in all of Asia, where people are now all talking about increasing Asian connectivity.

The investments of these new banks are going into exactly the sectors that were denied for decades by the International Monetary Fund (IMF) and the World Bank—namely into infrastructure. And all of these countries are thirsty and hungry for exactly these kinds of developments. Many countries have recently expressed interest in becoming transport hubs for the New Silk Road and the Maritime Silk Road. Indonesia wants to become a hub. Sri Lanka, Afghanistan, Iran. The New Silk Road is moving very, very rapidly in all of Eastern Europe. Just now, when President Xi Jinping was in Prague on a state visit to the Czech Republic, President Zeman praised the New Silk Road and emphasized the role of Prague, the Golden City, as the gateway between Europe and China. The 16+1 countries have just met in Riga, Latvia—these are the 16 East European and Central European countries—and they all want to be connected to the One Belt, One Road policy.

So this is moving very, very positively.

Trans-Atlantic Desperation

You contrast that with the trans-Atlantic sector: The too-big-to-fail banks of Wall Street and London are completely bankrupt, and faced with an immediate financial crash—much, much worse than what happened in 2008, a crash in which the entire $2 quadrillion in outstanding derivatives could blow up at any minute. Furthermore, the so-called tools of the central banks no longer function. As a matter of fact, every time a central bank does something to correct the problem, it boomerangs and has the opposite effect, as in the case of the Bank of Japan, of Norway, or the European Central Bank. When they go to zero interest rates, or even negative interest rates, it furthers the deflationary collapse instead of stimulating the real economy.

Just how desperate the situation in the trans-Atlantic system is, can be seen from the talk of the head of the European Central Bank, Mario Draghi, about helicopter money. Now that was, if you remember, an invention of Federal Reserve Chairman Ben Bernanke—the idea that, to avoid a meltdown of the entire financial system, you just fly helicopters over cities and throw down money, as much as is needed to prevent a melt-

The fact is that the unipolar world has already ceased to exist. It is a fact that China is rising; the United States is losing its hegemony. China is already exporting many more technologies than the United States. It is educating far more scientists and engineers, and the word in the science community internationally is, if you want to get anything done in frontier science, the place to go is China.

down. Now this obviously has caused a complete uproar in Germany, because people in Germany remember what the hyperinflation of 1923 was all about.

Then look at the condition of Europe. Look at the refugee crisis, which is not being discussed much. But the reality is that it is the result of the wars conducted mostly by the United States and the British in the Middle East, wars which were all based on lies. Iraq—no weapons of mass destruction. The war against Libya was initiated by a lie in the UN Security Council that it would not be a war. Look at Afghanistan: Was September 11 really as it was presented? Look at the situation in Yemen and in many African states.

The refugee crisis, the biggest humanitarian crisis probably since the end of the Second World War—condemning so many to unbelievable fates—has revealed that there is no European Union (EU), because there is no union. There is no unity. There is no solidarity. You have now a situation in which children are stuck behind barbed wire and police are shooting at them, trying to force them back. And then there is an absolutely shameful deal between the European Union and Turkey which—according to documents just delivered to the UN Security Council—is still supporting ISIS.

In Germany politicians are saying, "Oh, now we have fewer refugees." Yes, but at what price? They are being deported on a grand scale from internment camps in Greece, and it is a complete disgrace. Even the UN

UNHCR/I. Prickett

Refugees fleeing certain death are being deported on a grand scale from internment camps in a complete violation of human rights.

Human Rights Commission said this is a complete violation of human rights. It violates the Geneva convention on refugees. And all the aid organizations have already left because, they say, under the prevailing conditions, they cannot do their work. Doctors without Borders, for example, and many others.

The 'Clean Hands' Game

So the world is clearly in a complete mess, in a condition of disintegration, and what is the answer of the leading institutions of the trans-Atlantic sector? They have just pulled a big rabbit out of the hat called the Panama Papers. Now, one year ago, an anonymous source—such anonymity is always dubious—gave to the *Süddeutsche Zeitung* 11.5 million documents, which contained 40 years of data concerning the firm in Panama called Mossack Fonseca, which specializes in creating letterbox firms for the purpose of tax evasion. The International Consortium of Investigative Journalists then deployed 400 reporters in 80 countries for one year—financed by whom? By George Soros. The documents target politicians, industry leaders, sportsmen, and others.

Immediately, naturally, the focus was on Putin, even though his name is nowhere to be found in these documents, and on Xi Jinping. The *New York Times* has not wasted a day since the release, promoting this attack on Xi Jinping.

Let's look at this operation: What is this? Jürgen

Mossack, one of the founders, is the son a member of Hitler's Waffen SS. Ramón Fonseca Mora, the other guy, is the former president of the Panameñista Party, a party founded by Arnulfo Arias Madrid, an open Hitler supporter. The party was actively involved in the overthrow of General Noriega. The old Mossack was a member of the Nazi Waffen SS and after the war, offered his services to the U.S. government as an informant. Now that is entirely the profile of the Dulles brothers' famous rat line, by which they transported Nazis from Germany via the rat line to South America, to deploy them there for other purposes.

The focus on Xi Jinping is obviously especially ridiculous, because if there is one political leader in the world who is conducting an anti-corruption campaign in a completely ruthless fashion, then it is him. So, what is the purpose of this? Obviously, it is part of the present, trans-Atlantic hybrid warfare against Russia and China, with the aim of regime change by a variety of means: color revolutions using NGOs financed by foundations that are probably in this tax-exempt scheme; sanctions; and now the Panama Papers with the obvious hope of steering an uproar among the respective populations.

And it has almost worked in the case of the Icelandic President—people are now gathered in front of the residence of President Olafur Grimsson—but this m.o. is really not a new one. The way this has been functioning for a very long time is, you use certain assets owned by the governments, or secret services, and allow criminal operations and behavior to go on for a very long time. And then, at a convenient moment, you blow it up, and you cause a shake-up.

This was done very efficiently in the 1990s in Italy, with an operation called "Clean Hands," a national juridical investigation into political corruption that blew up the political system, ending the so-called First Republic of Italy, because all the parties were implicated. Anybody who has travelled to Italy knows that the entire postwar system of Italy was based on a principle called *"amici di amici."* You may not approve of it, but that's what it was: You couldn't get a job done without some kickback, and public works would always involved some bribes. The whole operation of bribes for public works was called *Tagentopoli*, or in English, "Bribesville." At that time, it involved 5,000 public figures and half of the Italian parliament. More than 400 city and town councils were dissolved, and the annual bribe rate in the 1990s was estimated to be $4 billion.

Now, Bloomberg recently reported that the Brazilian "anti-corruption" campaign against Dilma Rousseff, one of the BRICS leaders, is based on the Italian model. It is called "Operation Carwash."

So what they do is, they operate by a system of plea bargains, turning mafia bosses into snitches, and that way, you can roll up the whole political system. Now what comes out there is very interesting, because it reveals the total criminal character of the entire trans-Atlantic financial system. In the case of Mossack Fonseca—which is only the fourth largest of such firms, so one has to assume that there are many, many more such cases—it turns out that the HongShang bank [Hongkong and Shanghai Banking Corporation, HSBC] is responsible for 20% of these letterbox firms, and then comes the Union Bank of Switzerland and Crédit Suisse. And almost all the German banks are involved.

So what do you do when you have such a problem? The only way to stop this is, obviously, what Franklin D. Roosevelt did in 1933, when he obtained the Glass-Steagall Act requiring separation of the banks, simply bankrupting the fraudulent parts, and that is exactly what is required today: You need to separate the banks, protecting the commercial banking operations and closing down the derivatives, the toxic waste paper. Then you need a Pecora Commission to look into who committed what crime, and for what purpose.

Now, the funny thing is that when British Chancellor of the Exchequer George Osborne was asked, what about the fact that the father of Prime Minister David Cameron is also now a target in the Panama Papers, he said, "Oh, that is a private matter"! So it is quite amazing what nerve these people have.

So, the FDR solution for the United States. Then, we need to put down all of these crises, and I think it is absolutely feasible, but one has to take the path demonstrated by the negotiations between Secretary of State John Kerry and Foreign Minister of Russia Sergey Lavrov, in the case of Syria. There has to be a political agreement.

The Ideal Moment is Now!

But then, you need a *huge* development program. You need to do exactly what President Xi Jinping offered when he was in Iran, namely, to extend the New Silk Road—the One Belt, One Road policy—into the entire Middle East. Because you will not stop terrorism by dropping more bombs! If you launch more drones and drop more bombs, for every terrorist killed you will

The investments of these new banks are going into exactly the sectors that were denied for decades by the International Monetary Fund (IMF) and the World Bank—namely into infrastructure.

create a hundred new ones who hate the West even more than before.

So that is no solution. Obviously, ISIS has to be fought, and has to be gotten rid of, but you need a development perspective for the entire region, from Afghanistan to the Middle East, to the Mediterranean, and from the Caucasus to the Persian Gulf. And we need to wage war on the desert: We have to have a new source of fresh water, which is eminently possible with peaceful nuclear energy and desalination of large amounts of ocean water. We need to build new cities and develop agriculture and industry, so that the people of Syria, and Iraq, and Afghanistan, and Yemen, and Tripoli in Libya, and many, many African countries, have a future!

Why can we not take the offer of Xi Jinping to enter into a win-win cooperation with the large neighbors of the Middle East, Russia, China, India, Iran, and Egypt, and build up the Middle East in a Marshall Plan/New Silk Road fashion? The only reason why I mention the Marshall Plan, is that it reminds people that you can rebuild war-torn regions with a crash program. I know that China doesn't want to use this word, because the Marshall Plan has such a Cold War connotation; but we need to have a New Silk Road perspective.

The same applies, obviously, to settling the Ukraine crisis. You have probably heard that yesterday, the Dutch people voted in a referendum against the EU Association Agreement for Ukraine. This is very, very good: It means that this horrible EU is one step closer to its dissolution because, if you remember, it was the EU Association Agreement which was supposed to be signed by Yanukovych in late 2013 at the summit in Vilnius that started the whole Ukraine crisis.

Yanukovych realized at the last moment that because it would have given NATO total access to the territory of Ukraine, it would have made possible economic warfare against Russia, because of its border with Russia and the agreements between Ukraine and Russia. So at the last moment he did not sign. Then you had the color revolution, the Maidan events, all of these things developed. If you look at the chronology of these events, it was not Russia acquiring the Crimea; in every single instance, Russia reacted to a provocative action by NATO and by the EU, including a fascist coup in Ukraine in February 2014.

So if you want to solve this problem now? Well, this is the ideal moment, because the EU Association Agreement with Ukraine has just detonated, and it cannot be implemented. The results, announced today, of a Dutch referendum on whether to support that agreement, 61% of the voters were opposed. Even though only 32% of the Dutch people voted, the Netherlands government does not dare to go along with it, because there are many people in the 68% who did not vote who don't like the EU, because remember, Netherlands and France were the only two countries who voted *against* the EU Constitution in 2005.

So the ferment against this dictatorship which the EU has become, is just too big. And the lament today in the European media about the failure of this agreement is just absolutely loud and noisy.

OK. Let's use this situation, where, if there is one veto, this agreement cannot go through, let's use it to say: "Stop the confrontation with Russia!" Extend the European Union and the Eurasian Economic Union of Russia into one Eurasian area from the Atlantic to the Sea of China. Let's extend the Silk Road perspective to

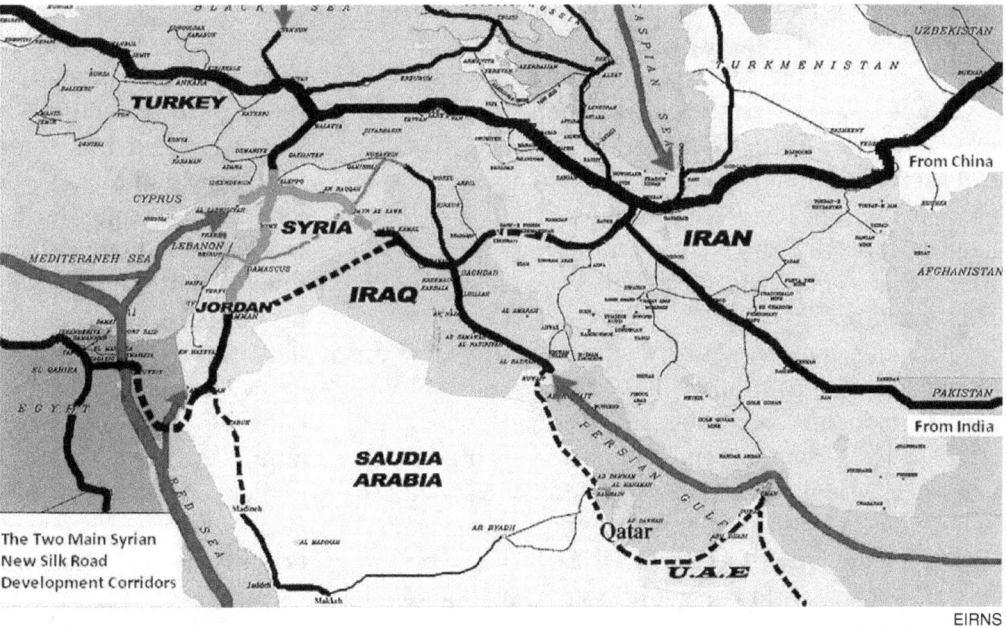

Maps depict routes for extending the New Silk Road Land-Bridge development corridors throughout the Middle East. Such a huge development perspective "from Afghanistan to the Middle East, to the Mediterranean, and from the Caucasus to the Persian Gulf," is the only way to eliminate regional conflict and the resultant refugee crisis.

include Ukraine and develop it! Because Ukraine is economically absolutely finished! The people are living a horrendous life as the result of what has happened in the last three years.

Let's do the same thing for Africa. Do people really think that we can sit there, and the 1% of the rich become richer and richer, by means which we now get a better window on with the Panama Papers, and the majority of the people lose everything? The middle class become the poor, and the poor have shortened lives. The gap between rich and poor worldwide is becoming bigger and bigger, and one billion people go hungry every day.

Klaus Schwab, the director of the Davos Economic Forum, said a couple of months ago that if present trends do not change, it is expected that *one billion people* will come as refugees to Europe in the next years. If it comes to that, and you have the effort to use NATO and Frontex—military ships—to fire on the refugees to try to deter them, what remains then of the "European values"? What about our humanism? What about *any* value?

So why don't we take the New Silk Road and say, "We now have a very attractive economic model which is already functioning very well in 60 nations of the world, so let us join hands, the United States, and Russia, and China, and European nations, and develop Africa." This is the moment at which we have to have a grand vision to change the plight of so many people.

Right now in Germany, there is one minister, the Development Minister Gerd Müller, who has travelled extensively in Southwest Asia and Africa, and who is now saying repeatedly—it's a big step forward—"we need a Marshall Plan, we need to develop these countries, because otherwise, they will bring all their problems to Europe."

And let's convince Japan that it is not in its interest to be drawn into military adventures against China. Japan is a country very much like Germany, which has almost no raw materials and achieved a very high living standard through high rates of investment in science and technology and by exporting. For Japan, the natural export market is all of Asia and Africa. It should be part of such a new world economic system and not go the way the Bank of Japan is now going, to zero interest rates, negative interest rates, and plunging deeper and deeper into the deflation.

And the United States?

Is the United States so much above the need for a New Silk Road? If you travel the roads from Washington to New York, or even on the roads in New York,— I don't understand why the citizens are not in an uprising against about the condition of these roads! They are so bad, that the roads in East Germany—at the end, before it collapsed—were smooth compared to what you have here! So the United States would obviously profit from joining the New Silk Road, in building infrastructure!

China had built 20,000 km of fast-train railroads by the end of last year, and it plans to have 50,000 km by 2025 or 2030, in any case, in a very short period of time. And the United States has built how many miles of fast-train railroads? Zero!

The New Silk Road is moving very, very rapidly in all of Eastern Europe. Just now, when President Xi Jinping was in Prague on a state visit to the Czech Republic, President Zeman praised the New Silk Road and emphasized the role of Prague, the Golden City, as the gateway between Europe and China.

So we propose that the United States—rather than wasting its industrial capacity in an ever-growing military-industrial complex, trying to militarize the whole world—should transform these industries and build fast trains, build maglev trains, or import the Chinese fast-train system, which is *excellent*. It's smooth, it's quick, and it doesn't shake at all like the European fast trains. So build 50,000 miles of fast train railroads in the United States! Fight the desert in the Southwest of the United States! Build a couple of new cities, you know? Large parts of the United States are completely undeveloped. Basically, after Teddy Roosevelt, no new cities were built in the West. Build some "smart cities," modern cities based on modular systems, but make *beautiful* cities! That would be a real challenge, to build beautiful cities, and not more Houstons. [applause]

We have put this program on the table: *The New Silk Road Becomes the World Land-Bridge.*

One reason we have proposed development for the entire world is that multipolarity is not the answer to a unipolar world. If you have multiple poles—groups of nations which still maintain their interests against other groups of nations—you still have the seed of geopolitics. And geopolitics is what caused two world wars in the Twentieth Century; if we were to come to a new world war, it would result in the annihilation of all mankind. The idea that you can have a *limited* war somewhere in the Pacific or somewhere in Europe, is complete bunk. All the military experts we have talked to, top-level military in Europe, the United States, and elsewhere, are convinced that it is in the nature of the

NTSB

The United States is in dire need of the development benefits that would be supplied by the New Silk Road development initiative. Above, site of the deadly Amtrak train wreck in Philadelphia, May 12, 2015.

existence of thermonuclear weapons, that it would come to a general, global war, if you start a war somewhere.

We need to replace geopolitics with a new paradigm, a paradigm which must be as different as was the Middle Ages from what we call "modern times." The Middle Ages was the time of scholasticism, superstition, the flagellants, people just going crazy, believing in Aristotle; and when Nicholas of Cusa and other great thinkers organized the Italian Renaissance, they designed a completely new paradigm which defined the role of the individual in a completely different way. It established the sovereign nation-state devoted to the common good for the first time; it made scientific and artistic progress possible in ways absolutely unknown before.

And we need, today, a completely new paradigm. If we cannot lift our thinking above the present, petty, so-called self-interest, the so-called "national interest," or really the interest of the big corporations and Wall Street, then we will not survive as a human species. What we need is an image of man, which is of man as the only creative species—to the best of our knowledge so far. In the Chinese Confucian philosophy, there is the word or the notion of *ren*, which is almost the same thing as the concept of *agape*, of love, in Christian humanism: that you have to have love for, and sustain harmonious relations with your family, your neighbor, your nation, and the international community of nations.

Now, the human species has come a very long way

in a very short period of time. If you think about the last 10,000 years, we have produced quite a number of great minds: Confucius, Plato, Mencius, Nicholas of Cusa, Kepler, Leibniz, Bach, Schiller, Beethoven, Tagore, Vernadsky, and Einstein, just to name a few—and that is how people should be.

A 'New Normal'

Now, you say, "These are people who are so extraordinary, that they only come once in a century." I don't think so. If we go now for the kind of reform that we are talking about, and you eliminate poverty, then no child, no person on the entire planet would be deprived of his or her basic needs. Then give all the children of this planet a universal education, giving them access to the great discoveries of the past; teach them Classical art; give them the kind of morality which used to be associated with Christian humanism, or with Buddhism, or with Confucianism, or other great cultures of this planet. The elimination of hunger and poverty is the best possible step for human rights! Because being poor and hungry does not allow you to exercise your human rights.

So if we take this road and say, Let's have a plan of global development, let's stop geopolitical wars, let's join hands to work together—so that every child of the future can have a perspective to become a scientist, to become a teacher, an artist, to become an astronaut or some other beautiful thing that develops the human mind—then, I think we need to go back to the high traditions of our own cultures. The Americans have to become republicans again, like the Founding Fathers—Benjamin Franklin, Alexander Hamilton—and like Lincoln, Roosevelt, and Kennedy. In Germany we need to go back to the German Classics. In other nations, we have high points of culture, which we have to revive.

And then we have to relate to each other from the standpoint of the highest form of our culture, and relate to the highest form of the culture of the other nation.

Then we will have a human world.

We should not give up on the idea that mankind is human! And that is what we have to fight for right now. So I think, if we do that—to speak in contemporary English—the "new normal" will be that every person is a genius.

Every Day Counts In Today's Showdown To Save Civilization

That's why you need EIR's **Daily Alert Service**, a strategic overview compiled with the input of Lyndon LaRouche, and delivered to your email 5 days a week.

For example: On Jan. 7, EIR's Daily Alert featured the British hand behind the pattern of global provocations toward war. Of special note is British Intelligence's role in instigating the Saudi Kingdom's attempt to set off a Sunni-Shia war. This religious war has been the intent of British strategy since the Blair-Bush attack on Iraq in 2003.

We also uniquely update you regularly on the progress toward the release of the suppressed 28 pages of the Congressional Inquiry on 9/11, which would expose the Saudi role.

Every edition highlights the reality of the impending financial crash/bail-in policies that would realize the British goal of mass depopulation.

This is intelligence you need to act on, if we are going to survive as a nation and a species. Can you really afford to be without it?

THURSDAY, JANUARY 7, 2016

Volume 2, Number 97

EIR Daily Alert Service

P.O. Box 17390, Washington, DC 20041-0390

- British Crown Pushing War and Genocide in 2016
- Financial Mudslide Goes On; Monetarist Tyranny Gloats over Bail-Ins
- Moody's Downgrades Portugal's Novo Banco
- Puerto Rico's Default: It's Every Vulture for Himself
- Wide Glass-Steagall Debate Set Off Again by Sanders Speech
- MI6 Mouthpiece Evans-Pritchard Touts Persian Gulf Chaos
- North Korea Tests a Miniaturized Hydrogen Bomb
- Uighur Terrorists Found in Indonesia
- Foreign Investors Are Flocking In to China

EDITORIAL

British Crown Pushing War and Genocide in 2016

MESSAGES TO THE SCHILLER CONFERENCE

'Bringing the New Silk Road to the American Public Is of Utmost Importance'

From **U.S. state legislators, union officials, and others:**

Dear Conferees,

Good luck on today's important gathering. It is of utmost importance that we bring the development policies of the New Silk Road to the American public. The United States media is either blacking out or misreporting these crucial breakthroughs in global infrastructure development. This infrastructure expansion is being driven by the economic ideas implemented in the United States from Alexander Hamilton to Franklin Roosevelt. The United States should return to these same, groundbreaking policies that built our nation. We should again become the Temple of Hope and Beacon of Liberty for All Mankind. We must join with the nations of the Middle East, Asia—including Russia, China, and India—and Latin America to build the urgently needed infrastructure projects that can rescue our imperiled civilization. Joint development . . . can be the basis for peace on our troubled planet.

We wish you all the success at today's conference.

Rep. Rodney Alexander, former member, U.S. Congress, 2003-2013, 5th CD, La.

Sen. Marilyn Moore, Chair, Senate Human Services Committee; Majority Whip, Bridgeport, Conn.

Rep. Edwin Vargas, House Appropriations Committee; former President, National Congress for Puerto Rican Rights; former President, Greater Hartford Labor Council, AFL-CIO; former Chairman, Hartford Democratic Party; Hartford, Conn.

Sen. Louis DiPalma, Vice Chairman, Senate Committee on Finance; the Physics First Advisory Board; Middletown, R.I.

Sen. Frank Ciccone, Vice Chairman, Senate Committee on Labor; Field Representative, Rhode Island Laborers District Council; Providence, R.I.

Sen. Dominick Ruggiero, Senate Majority Leader, former Majority Whip, North Providence, R.I.

Sen. Troy Jackson (former), member Democratic National Committee, candidate for State Senate, Allagash, Maine.

Mr. Severin Beliveau, attorney, former Chairman, Maine Democratic Party, Augusta, Maine.

Sen. William Soules, Vice-Chair, Education Committee; former President, New Mexico School Boards Association, Las Cruces, N.M.

Sen. Carlos Cisneros, Vice-Chair, Senate Finance Committee, Questa, N.M.

Rep. Antonio Maestas, Judiciary Committee; Majority Whip, Albuquerque, N.M.

Rep. George Dodge, House Business and Employment Committee, Santa Rosa, N.M.

Rep. John Kowalko, House Labor Committee; former Recording Secretary and Treasurer, Machinists Local Lodge 687; Newark, Del.

Rep. Thomas Jackson, former Chair, House Agriculture Committee; Past President, Clarke County Education Association; Thomasville, Ala.

Rep. Leon Howard, Chairman, Committee on Medical, Military, Public, and Municipal Affairs; former Chair, South Carolina Legislative Black Caucus; Columbia, S.C.

Rep. Terry Alexander, Labor, Commerce, and Industry Committee; former President, Florence, S.C. NAACP; Florence, S.C.

Rep. Joe Adams, Ranking Member, Select Committee on State and Local Governments; former President, St. Louis County Municipal

League; former President, Missouri Municipal League; former member, Board of Directors, National League of Cities; St Louis, Mo.

Lamar Lemmons, member and former President, Detroit Board of Education; former member, House of Representatives; Detroit, Mich.

Michael Balls, member, Saginaw City Council; President, Wanigas Credit Union Board of Directors; former Executive Board member, UAW Local 699; former Chair, UAW Local 699 Human and Civil Rights Committee; Saginaw, Mich.

Eric Mays, member, Flint City Council; former Recording Secretary, UAW Local 699; Flint, Mich.

Jim Dixon, President, Springfield and Central Illinois Trades and Labor Council, Springfield, Ill.

Mitchell Ponce, Business Agent, Ironworkers Local 433, Los Angeles and Las Vegas; Industry, Calif.

Alex Cassas, Business Manager and Financial Secretary, IBEW Local 583; President, El Paso Building Trades Council; El Paso, Texas

Greg Lance, Legislative Committeeman, International Association of Machinists and Aerospace Workers Local 1725, Charlotte, N.C.

Tim Palmeri, Executive Vice President, Bricklayers Local 1, Wallingford, Conn.

Philip Prada, Spirit Airlines Pilot Association's Government Affairs Chairman; Captain, Airbus 320; Chicago, Ill.

Claretta Allen, Vice-President, Texas AFL-CIO, District 17; Recording Secretary, Smith County Central Labor Council; Tyler, Texas.

The following have sent individual messages, each characterized here by a brief excerpt.

Former U.S. Senator Mike Gravel, Alaska:

The Silk Road, in my mind, remains an opportunity for all nations, not only the BRICS, but all nations. And I hope and pray that the United States will eventually join this effort.

State Senator Richard Black, Virginia:

I have very deep reservations about what we're doing in Syria.

Ramasimong Phillip Tsokolibane, leader, LaRouche South Africa:

The world is watching your conference for signs that forces in the United States can be mobilized in time to bring your great nation back to its true historic mission, as a force for human progress, before it is too late.

Xolisa Mabhongo, Representative of the Director General of the International Atomic Energy Agency to the United Nations:

The IAEA in its work affords the world the opportunity to utilize peaceful nuclear technology in many fields including, energy, human health, food production, water management, and environmental protection. We transfer nuclear technology to developing countries around the world to help them achieve their development objectives.... Had I attended the conference, I would have elaborated on these and many other aspects of the IAEA's work.

Dr. Kelvin Kemm, CEO, Nuclear Africa, Pretoria, South Africa:

People of the vast Dark Continent want light, ... not from a motor car battery in a wooden box, with an attached solar panel, ... but from nuclear power stations. We want to see a dozen new cities arise in Africa, looking like new versions of London, New York, Paris, and Berlin. Great minds will be gathered in New York for the contemplation of the challenges in Building a World Land-Bridge.... Have fun. True achievement is exciting and exhilarating.

Dr. Panchapakesa Jayaraman, poet, scholar, and founder, Bharatiya Vidya Bhavan, New York Branch:

The Indian wise men—Sages—have given us numerous instructions for creating classical cultural unity within us. The following Hymn—Mantra from one of the first and foremost Indian scriptures, Yajurveda—is one among them. Can we not easily follow this principle for creating Peace within us? [The hymn:] 'May all beings look on me with the eye of a friend! May I look on all beings with the eye of a friend! May we look on one another with the eye of a friend!'

LI XIGUANG

Creating a Dialogue of Cultures on the New Silk Road

by William Jones

April 10—Speaking at the Schiller Institute conference in New York on April 7, Professor Li Xiguang, the director of the Tsinghua University Center for International Communication Studies, engrossed his audience in the saga of his extraordinary quarter-century of total personal devotion, as a leading Chinese personality, to the New Silk Road project. Professor Li brought the New Silk Road proposal of China's President Xi Jinping, the so-called "Belt and Road," vividly to life. Over 26 years, Professor Li has travelled the Silk Road with no fewer than 500 of his students.

While the proposals of the Silk Road Economic Belt through Central Asia, and the 21st Century Maritime Silk Road through South and Southeast Asia, have a predominantly economic content, they are also strategically important for China as its political influence grows, Professor Li noted. The hostile attitude taken by the United States to China's long-suppressed maritime territorial claims, mobilizing the U.S. Navy and the forces of its military allies in the region,— including a revitalized Japanese force projection,— is an attempt by the United States to create a strategic "cordon sanitaire" along the Pacific Rim, in which patrolling U.S., Japanese, Australian, and Filipino naval vessels will potentially threaten to cut off China's free access to the surounding seas.

Access to the Oceans

Faced with this problem, Professor Li explained, China is concentrating on creating ocean access toward the West and Southwest, preparing to build major ports in the Indian Ocean and Arabian Sea in Sri Lanka, Bangladesh, Myanmar, and Pakistan. While the United States is also doing its best to rally these countries in its attempt to limit growing Chinese influence there, these nations are not engaged, as are Japan, the Philippines, and Australia, in a direct military alliance with the

EIRNS/Stuart Lewis

Professor Li Xiguang addressing the April 7 Schiller Institute conference.

United States. Even India, which is being heavily courted by the United States as a hedge against China, is presently not a military ally of the United States, and has had, in spite of recent tensions, a long-term political and cultural relationship with China.

"Helga talked about a South China Sea potential war, and China worries about a potential conflict with U.S. and other naval maneuvers in the South China Sea, and worries about an American naval blockade of the Malacca Straits," Professor Li said. "So China wants to have a new Maritime Silk Road which will not pass through the Malacca Strait, and as a result, China is now building four ports in countries along the Indian

Ocean. One is the Kyaukpyu port in Myanmar, another the Chittagong port in Bangladesh, Colombo port in Sri Lanka, and Gwadar port in Pakistan. And so far, China has completed construction in Colombo, Sri Lanka, and also the Gwadar port in Pakistan.

"And this is the ancient Silk Road. In China, the explorer Faxian (337-422) is a household word, and even more so Xuanzang (602-664), who was a Tang Dynasty Buddhist monk. He traveled from Xian, Xi Jinping's home province, through China's Xinjiang Province, climbed over the Tian Shan Mountains, and walked into Uzbekistan, Tajikistan, Bukhara, and Khorezm, and through Afghanistan and through today's Pakistan into India. He spent something like 15 years on the road. And eventually he brought back 600 copies of Buddhist scriptures on elephants and on horses. And that is why Xian was so famous, because it has the oldest stupa, or Buddhist pagoda, built for this monk."

(Xuanzang's trip was made more difficult by the necessity, in the Tang Empire, to obtain permission to travel abroad, which the lone monk did not have. But in spite of the obstacles, he was determined to travel to India and bring its lessons back to China. His trip is also widely known through the somewhat fanciful description, based only roughly on Xuanzang's actual adventure, of the famous Ming Dynasty novel, *Journey to the West*. There a Monkey King becomes the monk's guide, taking him through all sorts of miraculous adventures. It is considered one of the Four Great Classical Novels of Chinese literature. The story, retold in film and on television as well as in children's books, is known and loved by all Chinese children.)

Twenty-six Years on the Silk Road

Professor Li certainly knows whereof he speaks, since he has traveled extensively over the route of Xuanzang, and the entire Belt and Road region, for the last 26 years. "In 1990, that is 26 years ago, when I was a young scholar of the UNESCO Silk Road Project, I started my journey following the footsteps of Xuanzang of the Tang Dynasty. Ever since then I have been travelling and writing on the Silk Road, as a journalist and also as a journalism educator."

Since then Li Xiguang has also taken many of his students on trips to the Silk Road regions; he showed the Schiller Institute conference many pictures of sites they had visited along the ancient Silk Road. "And in this winter vacation, a month ago," he said, "I took our students to Kolkata in eastern India, and also Bangla-

desh. This was a really hard-travelling class; the students were so tired that at night they slept on the bus. Except me: I just kept a watchful eye on the driver; the Bangladesh drivers were crazy. [laughter] So I had to talk to him constantly so he would not fall asleep like the students."

Professor Li identified three main corridors moving down through South Asia. The first, and the one that is most advanced presently, is the China-Pakistan Economic Corridor (CPEC). "It goes through the western part of the Himalayan Mountains, that is, the Hindu Kush Mountains and the Karakoram Mountains," Professor Li explained. "And China had already built a highway there in the early 1970s [see map, p. 39], but China and Pakistan are planning to build a railway and a gas pipeline along this Karakoram Highway. And the Karakoram Highway, starting from China's westernmost city, Kashgar, now ends in Islamabad, Pakistan. But the corridor will be further extended through Pakistan's Khyber Pashtu province and Gilgit-Baltistan region, all the way to Gwadar port in Pakistan."

The second route is the China-India-Bangladesh-Myanmar Corridor. But a lack of firm commitment on the part of India—under intense U.S. pressure—to develop this corridor, has been an obstacle. "And Bangladesh gave some support originally," Li said. "The Chittagong port construction has been signed and China has sent its construction team there, but according to Indian press reports two months ago, it was suddenly stopped by the Bangladesh government. The Bangladesh government decided to cooperate with Japan to build a new port only 25 km from the Chinese-planned port in Chittagong. And India is strongly against this Chittagong port, regarding it as something in India's backyard." The third corridor is the China-Tibet Railway corridor, which now ends near the Nepal and Indian border.

A Proposed Cultural Belt

Given the difficulties presented by U.S. hostility, Li has proposed a Cultural Silk Road Belt along with the Economic Belt. "What is the basis for the Cultural Belt along the Silk Road?" he asked. "Actually, the British sources—I mean the academic sources doing research about the Silk Road—the American sources, Indian sources, and Chinese sources, they all have their sources in Chinese books by Faxian, by Xuanzang, by all these monks; they're more accurate, actually than Marco Polo's records.

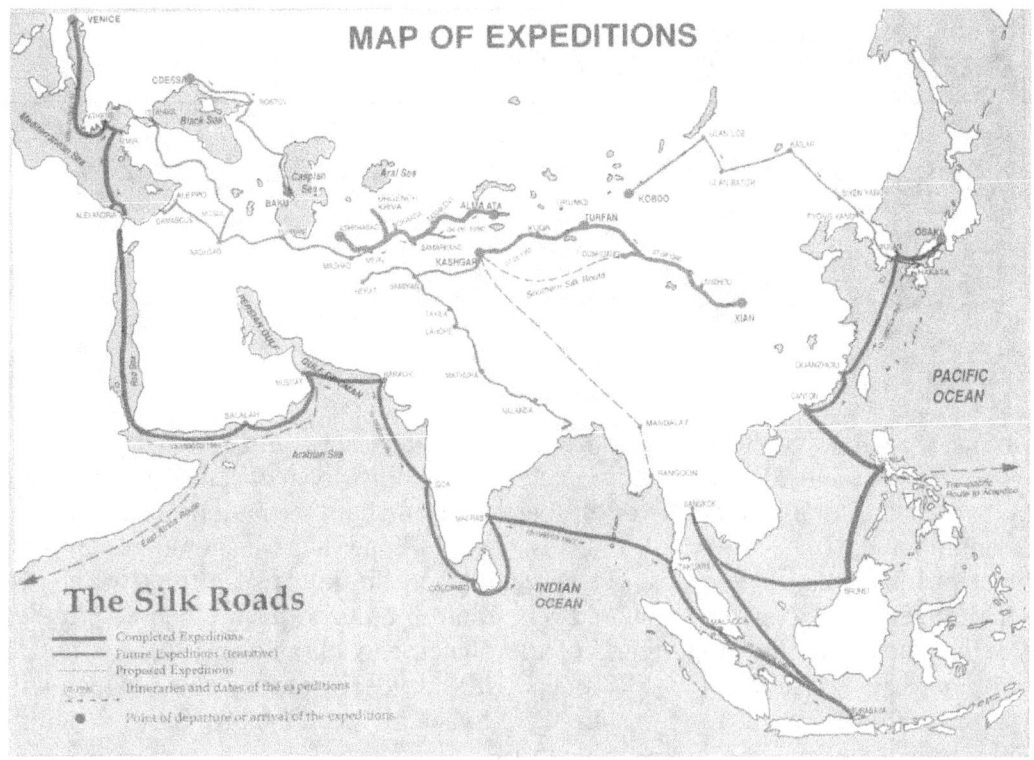

MAP OF EXPEDITIONS

The Silk Roads

Completed Expeditions
Future Expeditions (tentative)
Proposed Expeditions
Itineraries and dates of the expeditions
Point of departure of arrival of the expeditions

Professor Li Xiguang

Portions of the ancient Chinese silk routes that have been traversed by Professor Li Xiguang over the past 26 years, accompanied by no fewer than 500 of his students.

common. So if we utilize these common things we share, they could serve to build a Cultural Belt.

"And Xi Jinping in his official statement said that he wants to build a Silk Road, and he said that top priority for China's foreign policy is to build a community of common interests of neighboring countries and China," Li continued. "That has been interpreted by some Chinese scholars, as being different from the policy of previous Chinese leadership; the previous leadership regarded Chinese-American relations as the top priority. But now we regard the building of a community of common interests of neighboring Asian countries as the top priority in foreign policy. And I also said it is a community of common faith. But in my study, I proposed that the base for a community of common faith and community of common interests, should be a community of common value, a community of common security, and a community of common culture—a big culture, not a small culture."

"So from reading these ancient source documents and also doing our own research, we found that we share more things in common than differences; I see more identical elements, instead of differences. Like India-China relations: Actually, one of the three key elements of Chinese culture is Buddhism. Buddhism comes from India. And with Pakistan. Pakistan is a Muslim country and China has 20 million Muslims, like in Xinjiang, in Gansu, in Ningxia, and Qinghai; these are all Muslim provinces very close to Pakistan. I regard this as a resource for the Belt and Road. I never regarded Muslims as bad elements, or as some potential threat. That's why Pakistan, actually, in the Chinese mind and in the Pakistani mind,— Pakistan and China are the closest allies. If China has one ally, it is Pakistan and no other country. That is totally different from American mentality in this regard.

"And we're also connected by Buddhism and by language with Central Asia, as China maintains a number of autonomous regions. With the Uzbeks, we have our own Uzbek autonomous region, and with Tajiks, who are Iranian-speaking people, we have our Iranian-language autonomous counties in Tashkurgan, in the westernmost region. So we share many things in

regard the building of a community of common interests of neighboring Asian countries as the top priority in foreign policy. And I also said it is a community of common faith. But in my study, I proposed that the base for a community of common faith and community of common interests, should be a community of common value, a community of common security, and a community of common culture—a big culture, not a small culture."

Li Xiguang has here given a firm confirmation of the need for what Helga Zepp-LaRouche has been calling for: transforming the "Belt and Road" into a new paradigm for mankind, a new paradigm in relations between cultures, building on the highest achievements of each of them. And the Schiller Institute conference in New York showed that there is the clear possibility of bringing the United States out of its enthrallment with a Cold War and British imperial mindset, and back to the traditions of Alexander Hamilton and John Quincy Adams, in which the nations of different cultures—and different forms of government—can, and must, work together to realize the common aims of mankind in economic development and mutual cultural enrichment.

II. The New Scientific Frontiers

MESSAGE OF LAROUCHE TO THE SCHILLER CONFERENCE

'To Give the People Spirit'

We've come to the point in history where we need new openings to the advising of man, in order to escape the kinds of threats which are taking over mankind or many parts of mankind, today.

We have to also, at the same time, realize that there has been a great demoralization among the people of nations, and that we have to be sensitive to what those problems are and to what the solutions are, for those purposes. I am actually disposed, to recognize what this problem is, and therefore, I will plead among people to recognize their option and ability and responsibility to create a new assembly of various parties, throughout the nations of the Earth.

And we should hope that we should come to an early agreement on the kinds of efforts which we should rely upon in order to inspire people in other parts of the planet, as well as our own, in order to give the people spirit, self-injected spirit, which will inspire them to actually lead the process of a victory for this cause.

Lyndon LaRouche in dialogue with conference participants during Panel II.

KESHA ROGERS

'A Restored NASA Mission Must Drive an Economic Renaissance'

Dennis Speed: Over the course of the past several weeks in particular, but actually in a different way over the course of at least the last several years, our keynote speaker for the afternoon has been a pioneer in attempting what some would think would be impossible, which is a resurrection of the spirit of America, as that spirit was best exemplified in the Apollo Project. It's important to think about the idea that the Apollo Project is not a technological success, merely, but it was a change in culture, and it was a change from the pessimism of the time of the Cold War to the possibility, not only of world peace, but of a new economic, scientific, and cultural platform for all of mankind.

We all walked on the Moon, on July 20, 1969. And so, in order that we might restore that idea today, we have with us Kesha Rogers, from Houston, former Democratic Party Congressional candidate, to tell us why "A Restored NASA Science Mission Must Drive an Economic Renaissance."

Kesha Rogers: Thank you, Dennis, and I bring you greetings from the soon-to-be beautiful city of Houston, Texas. I want to start off this afternoon's panel by saying, first of all, that I think that the message that Mr. La-Rouche just conveyed, gets at the very heart of the conception of what we must seek to create, as the basis for a peaceful and productive future for all of mankind,— which requires all nations working together to realize the creative potential and spark of every child, and every human being. And those of you who were here for the panel discussion this morning can really testify to the fact that that was the essence of this morning's panel, and of what you should take from the entirety of this conference, as the essence of this conference,— and what we seek to take back out into our communities, and to humanity, as a new hope for the future of mankind.

Now the question that should be posed today, is

Stuart Lewis/EIRNS

"The question that should be posed today," said Kesha Rogers, "is what must be the true purpose and mission of mankind's exploration of space?"

what must be the true purpose and mission of mankind's exploration of space? The importance of the space program lies in the very fundamental conception of realizing mankind's true humanity. That human beings are not mere animals, but are creative beings. And my conception of the space program is that we have to renew it as the pinnacle of a true renaissance, and a true paradigm, a new paradigm for mankind.

Now, that means that we have to, once and for all, take the lid off scientific progress. In order to accomplish this goal, we must increase our understanding of mankind as a space-faring species. And mankind must realize once again, what the great pioneer of space, Krafft Ehricke, deemed our "extraterrestrial imperative."

Now, when people think about the space program, they think, in many cases, of practical benefits: spin-offs and new technologies. And these are important,— but how are they achieved? Through a vision! And when you think about the essence of the visionary leadership of a pioneer such as Krafft Ehricke, and the conception that he developed in his idea of the extraterrestrial imperative of man, you see that he gets at something deeper, more fundamental, than just the creation of new technologies. He declared, "More profound and inspiring than the technologies, however, are human and social-economic implications, understood in the perspective of the extraterrestrial imperative. Space industrialization is the crucible in which the seemingly irreconcilable problems that cause such profound pessimism in the outlook of many can be resolved. Earth and space become one, through the intelligence and the creativity of man."

Attack on Man's Identity

Now take that conception of the creativity of man, and the true mission for which we should be fighting for a space program, and compare that to the problem which we face today in the attack on scientific progress, which has been a continuing policy coming from the Obama Administration. But you have to look at this from the standpoint that it's not a dispute over budgets or anything of that nature, but there's a fundamental attack on the human creative identity. And the policy that we're witnessing in the United States has been a direct frontal attack on scientific progress, on our space program, and on the true creativity that must be brought forth from every single human being. And that's the evil of dismantling what has been the unified mission for our space program. You can't call it anything but that,— evil.

To understand this threat more fully, I want you to think back to the day before President John F. Kennedy was shot. I would encourage people to go and listen to President Kennedy's speech of Nov. 21, 1963, in Houston, Texas,— a very powerful speech. In that speech, President Kennedy envisioned an "America strong in science and in space, in health and in learning, in respect of its neighbors and all nations,— an America that is both powerful and peaceful." "With a people," he added, "that are both prosperous and just." He concluded, "With that vision we shall not perish and we cannot fail."

That vision of President Kennedy is one that his British assassins have continued to strike down, have continued to reject as our human identity. Instead, they have pushed through a policy of cultural degeneracy, population reduction and mass suicide, and drugs, despair, homelessness, and hopelessness. They have sought to destroy President Kennedy's vision for peace among nations through development, through coopera-

NASA

Kennedy, in a speech in Houston, Texas, Nov. 21, 1963, said he envisioned an "America strong in science and in space, in health and in learning, in respect of its neighbors and all nations,— an America that is both powerful and peaceful." Here, Kennedy addresses a joint session of Congress, calling for the space program.

tion in scientific breakthroughs, and through a commitment to continued progress in space exploration. Having shut down our space program, Obama and the British Empire are now driving for total war.

The previous speakers have shown us the intention for a new paradigm, that is coming from nations, particularly China, and why China poses such a threat right now to the existence of Obama's culture of death, bestiality, and moral degeneracy, the attack on human progress. China is now bringing into being a new future for the progress of mankind. China's mission to explore the far side of the Moon embarks on new frontiers, on new discoveries which have yet to be accomplished. These will be discoveries that will not only benefit the progress of one nation, but all nations.

It is urgent that we in the United States return to the principles of a space program as a mission for all humanity, as the antithesis to the threat of nuclear war. We must continue to develop joint efforts of cooperation with Russia in space exploration, as well as developing new relationships of cooperation with China, and all the other great nations that have been represented at this conference—and more—to bring about a new paradigm for mankind.

I think that is the challenge that I would like to start this panel discussion with today, in response to what Mr. LaRouche has laid out as the inspiration that we as Americans—and we as a unified humanity—can bring about once again.

JASON ROSS

'We Aren't Done Yet'

Dennis Speed: During the period 1999, 2000, 2001, LaRouche created something called the LaRouche Youth Movement. He insisted that the difference would be that among those people that he was recruiting at that time, there had to be a scientific rigor, a sense of the knowledge of the way that the world really works, because that was the only way to really understand economics. To that end, there was a years-long project that was undertaken by many young people. First, an intensive study of the work of Johannes Kepler, followed by the work of Carl Gauss and that of Bernhard Riemann, among others.

In the course of doing that, something was created called the "Basement Team." This was a group of people who worked with LaRouche on a daily basis

EIRNS/Stuart Lewis
Jason Ross addressing the April 7 conference.

to probe and explore the frontiers of knowledge, not merely in terms of the sciences as the physical sciences, but in terms of the methodology: how do you think about these problems, how to approach these problems.

And so, to take us to that place where these matters rise above the level of simple hardware, to the level of the subjective mindset, creative mindset, that has to be the basis for our discovery of our place in the universe, I want to introduce Jason Ross, who has functioned as the editor of *21st Century Science & Technology* magazine, still available online; and is a member of, and leader of, the LaRouche Basement Team.

Jason Ross: Good afternoon! I am very glad to be here. I was going to title my presentation, "Science, as

Society's Unifying Mission," but in light of the discussion we've been having, I think a more appropriate title might be, "We Aren't Done Yet." I'll tell you what I mean by that.

I'd like to discuss the purpose of society as I see it, the purpose of the nation and its role with respect to its individuals, and the role that science plays in that—and use the discussion to incorporate a couple of Mr. LaRouche's economic principles, discoveries that he had worked on around the year 1950, and which led him to be the most successful economic forecaster today. Those familiar with his history will recall, perhaps as recently as a few years ago, or a decade ago, or go back to the dot.com bubble, that when all the "experts" were saying the dot.com bubble will never pop, LaRouche was right. When people said there would never be another recession, LaRouche was right. Now why was that? Let's talk about what economics is.

First, the goal of a society goes beyond ensuring the physical well being of its people. I am sure many of you are familiar with the various Freedoms of Franklin Roosevelt, such as the Freedom from Want and the Freedom from Fear. What about the Freedom from Anomie, the Freedom from Uselessness, the Freedom from Wondering Was That a Life Well Lived or Even Worth It At All? The mission that drives individuals, and that they can reflect on at the time of their passing, as having made them necessary and useful persons, comes in part from the decisions that they make, but also in very large degree from the decisions that the society as a whole makes, and the context in which they live out their lives.

For example, during the Apollo program, many components went into the spacecraft. Many of those components were produced with new manufacturing techniques. But I suspect that some of them might have come from the same kind of factory that produced parts for any other application. The people making those parts,— by their being engaged in an endeavor to go to the Moon and do something new for the species as a whole, the value of their work increased, insofar as it was part of that context. So, I want to keep that in mind, in terms of economics.

Potential Population Density

The opportunity to be able to provide citizens, to provide people a life on which they can look back and say that I think this is the highest mission of the nation; it's the highest mission of society, and it's one that we can collaborate on with all the other nations, in that it's a purely affirmative policy. It's not about superiority. It's not about maintaining power over others. It's about "what are we doing that's new?"

To discuss that, allow me to introduce a concept, "potential population density." Let me do it by asking a question. Around the world we know of a fair amount of corruption. We know of a fair amount of poor decisions that are being made, some intentional, some through neglect. The pursuit of a war policy by the Obama administration, as Helga has described in great detail, leading towards a confrontation with Russia and China—that's obviously a bad policy that should be overturned, repudiated.

Let's say that none of those problems existed. Let's say that we are running everything as well as we possibly could. The leaders of society are all concerned for people's well being. We are not stealing from each other. There's still a limit to how good living standards can be, and it's determined not just by the way we relate to each other, but by what we know about the world around us.

I want to do this by putting economics in terms of physical chemistry. Think about the number of people that could be supported, or who could live on an acre, or per square kilometer, 5,000 years ago. Let's say 6 or 7,000 years ago, actually. This is before the use of

metals; this is certainly before the use of power sources. There's a limit. The development of metallurgy 5,000 years ago, the opportunity to take something from the ground, a rock, and turn it into a metal, to make new kinds of tools—that transformed how we were able to live.

Consider the value of the steam engine, which came into major play about 200 years ago. The value of the introduction of the steam engine isn't something that a Wall Street banker could put a number value on.

The value of a society in which we are able to use chemical energy to create motion—that's something that transforms who we are. The potential there lies in the difference between physical power and chemical power. So, falling weights, moving around objects— there's a certain amount of power in that. When you have atoms that are bound together, and you change those atomic bonds, as in burning coal, for example, you can create heat. The heat is able to cause steam to expand and push a piston. You can turn that into motion. You've just turned a rock into motion!

What did that enable, in terms of transportation, with the railroads? What did it allow, in terms of production, with manufacturing? What did it allow, in terms of reducing the *physical* cost of producing goods for people and making them available to a broader part of the population, when they weren't made by hand or by a water wheel, but could be made by combustion?

Think about the higher level of nuclear power. Many people are scared of nuclear power, for reasons that don't exist, mainly because they have no understanding of what it means. The nucleus of an atom is bound together—protons and neutrons. By rearranging them, combining nuclei, separating them apart, you release energy. The amount of energy involved in nuclear bonds is a million times beyond what is possible with chemical power! And, it can do different things.

Just in terms of the numbers, think about the value to society in being able to mine five pounds of uranium, to provide all the energy needed for a person for a year, compared to 100,000 pounds of coal or oil. What's the physical cost involved in going through all that coal or oil, compared to those five pounds of uranium?

It's not just about the amount of energy; it's about what can you do with it. Let's look at the first slide

FIGURE 1
Electricity Consumption vs GDP, per capita

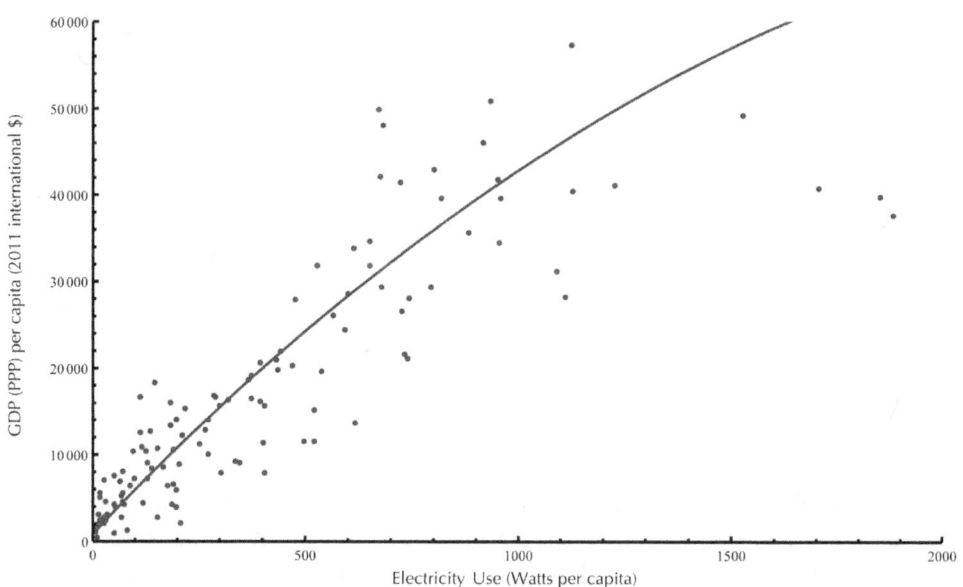

(**Figure 1**). This is a comparison. Gross Domestic Product (GDP) is not the ultimate economic value, but I think this really speaks for itself. Here's a chart. On the horizontal axis you have energy use per person, in various countries. And on the vertical axis, you have the GDP per person. This makes an obvious statement: Without power, you can't have improvement in standards of living; without power, you don't have development. So, the ability to provide that kind of power to people, of course that's a necessity for what we're doing.

Necessity of Nuclear Power

Going beyond that, we have to think about the quality of that power. Kesha Rogers referred to the speech that President Kennedy made about going to the Moon. There are other things that he discussed in that speech. There were other proposals that Kennedy made. One of them was for a nuclear rocket.

Let's take a look at the next slide. (**Figure 2**) This is the rocket that went to the Moon, the Saturn V. On the right you see its weight, almost entirely fuel. The dry

FIGURE 2

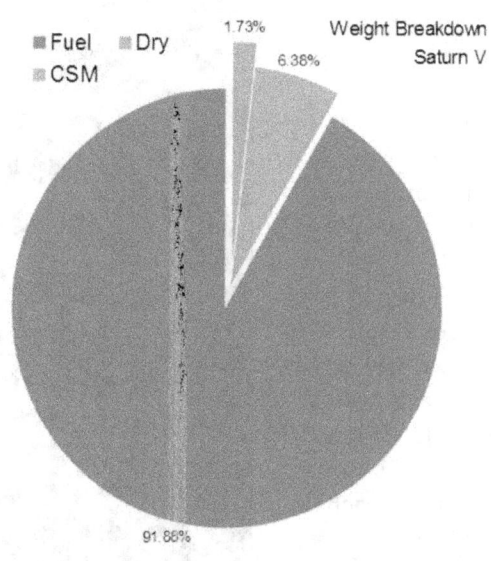

FIGURE 3

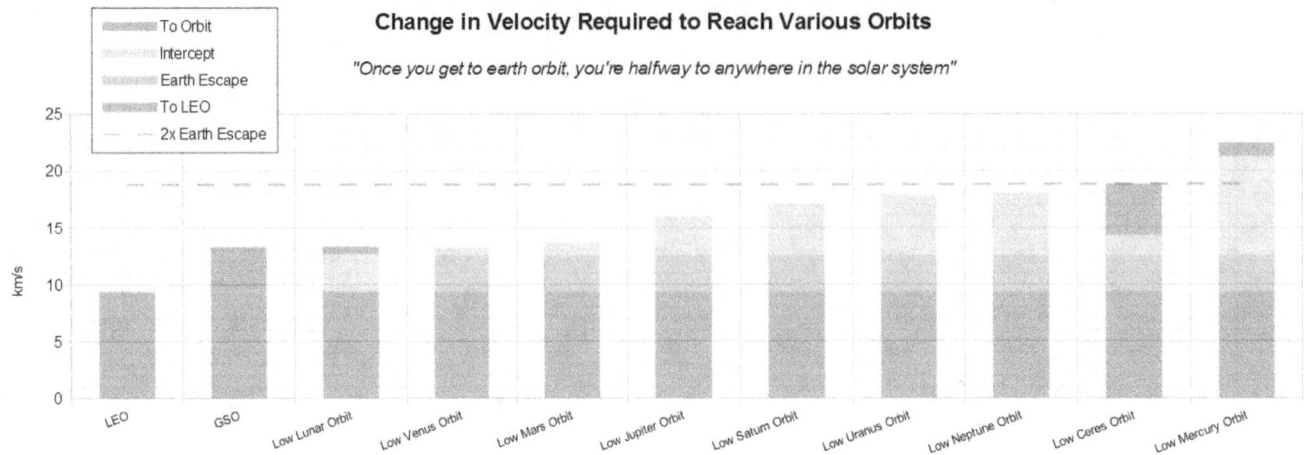

Change in Velocity Required to Reach Various Orbits

"Once you get to earth orbit, you're halfway to anywhere in the solar system"

portion of that pie graph refers to the structure required to hold the fuel. The reddish-orange section is what actually went to the Moon and came back. The rocket's weight is basically *nothing but fuel*, if you look at it that way. Certainly we've already reached the limits of what we can do in space with chemical propulsion.

Let's look at the next slide (**Figure 3**) which shows just the effort of getting off the ground. This is a chart of the amount of energy required to get to various places in the Solar System. The blue bar, which goes up to about nine, that's just the energy to get up off the ground, to get up off the Earth. Just getting off the Earth is half of what's required to get anywhere else. Without changes in the way that we relate to space, and how we are able to move around in it, we're not able to reach the next level.

Take a look at

the next slide. (**Figure 4**) Here's an example application. Asteroids strike the Earth. It happens. Eventually, an asteroid of a large enough size to kill everybody will strike the Earth. We've got a pretty good indication that it won't be within the next ten years, but we don't know where most of these asteroids are. When we find them, if one is coming towards us, we can't do anything about it if it's larger than a very, very small one. All we could

FIGURE 4

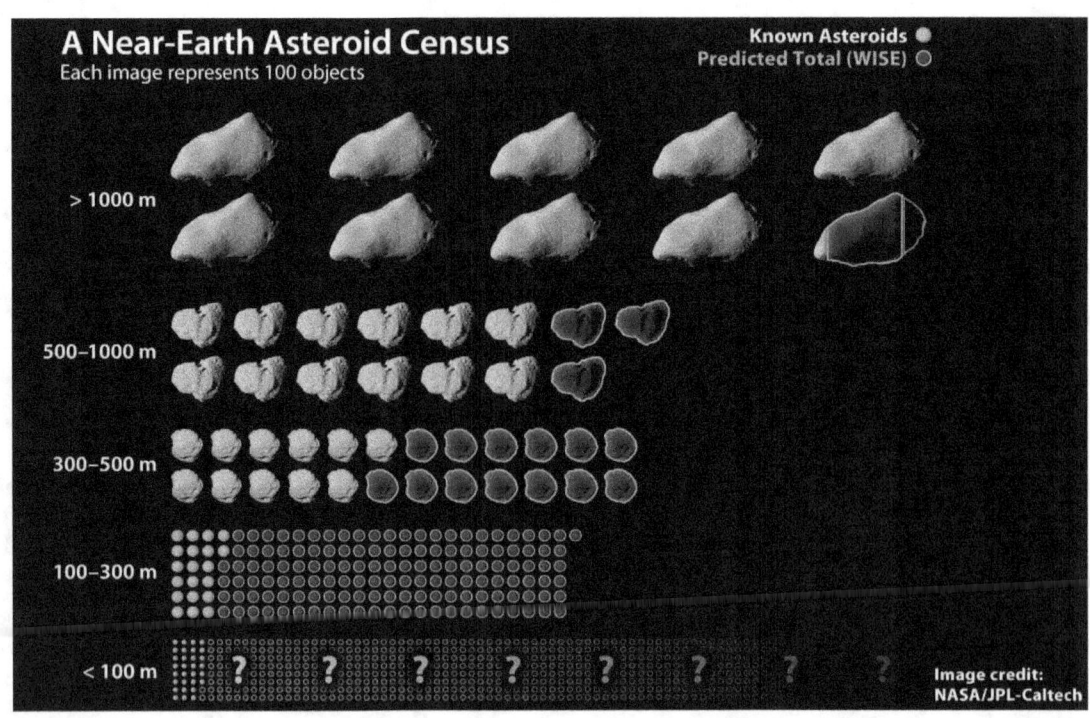

A Near-Earth Asteroid Census
Each image represents 100 objects

Known Asteroids ●
Predicted Total (WISE) ○

> 1000 m

500–1000 m

300–500 m

100–300 m

< 100 m

Image credit:
NASA/JPL-Caltech

FIGURE 5

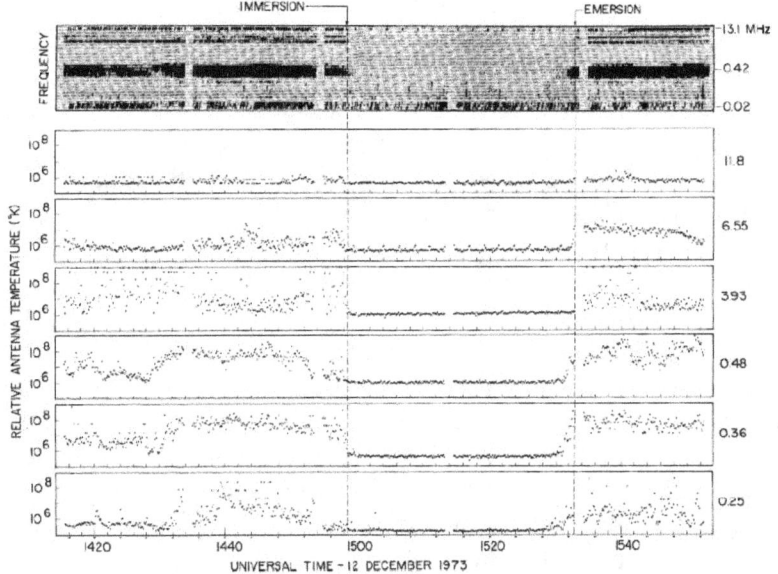

Example of a lunar occultation of the Earth as observed with the upper-V burst receiver of the lunar-orbiting RAE-2 satellite, from Alexander et al. *This shows the significance of the terrestrial noise even at the distance of the Moon, and its elimination behind the Moon.*

do would be to evacuate an area that it's going to hit. How are we going to be able to defend ourselves from threats like this? It is not going to be done with lower-level energy sources; it's not going to be done with chemical power; it's not going to be with the low energy-density of solar power. It is going to be done with the kind of intense power that you are able to concentrate by using nuclear fuels.

What Path to Progress?

One of the difficulties in looking at this, is that we think in terms of the present rather than the future. For example, the power required on the planet right now would be over ten times what it currently is, if everyone on the planet had the use of energy and a developing economy to go with it. That is where the United States would be today, had we not had the shift after the assassination of Kennedy, after that shift away from development. Had we not had that shift toward an absolute takeover by the Wall Street idea of value, where money is the measure of value, instead of our physical abilities, U.S. energy use right now would be double what it currently is. Around the world, you are talking ten or twenty times current world levels. The disparity be-

tween where we are right now and where we would be if we had we just continued, is enormous. Add in where we ought to be in the future, and it's absolutely tremendous.

Who is making that happen? Well, the role of the Chinese space program has been discussed a fair amount here. China, as people know, is the first nation to make a soft landing on the Moon in decades, with the Chang'e lander and the Yutu rover. China is planning, in 2018, to land on the far side of the Moon, something that *no* nation has ever done. I'll show you one picture of why that would be useful. (**Figure 5**) Going from left to right, we have time. This is a fly-by around the far side of the Moon. You can see the intensity of the [ambient] radio waves. Behind the Moon, you can see how low it gets. The only quiet place we're going to find to do new radio telescope work, to be able to look out and find new things about the universe, is on the far side of the Moon. It's protected from the Earth.

Think about what we learned with the Laser Interferometer Gravitational-Wave Observatory (LIGO) experiment, and the detection of those gravity waves that were predicted by Einstein 100 years ago. What that represents is a *new sense*, in terms of the five senses, a new way to "listen" to the universe, a new way to "look" at things. What kinds of further discoveries will that lead to in the future? What will it mean for us to learn more about the quantum world? In a certain way, even the "laws" of thermodynamics aren't true.

What are the first two laws of thermodynamics? The First Law—*untrue*—is that the total amount of energy in the universe is fixed. I bet a lot of people think that's true. When that "law" was passed, in the 1860s, nuclear power didn't exist. So, with the development of nuclear energy, with Einstein's $E = mc^2$, you say, "Well, OK, the amount of energy in the universe is still fixed, but now we have the right number; now we've figured it out." Well, are we done? Have we figured everything out? Of course not! We're not done!

The Second Law of Thermodynamics, that the universe tends towards disorder, that is the popular presentation of it, and the one I want to address: Again, it is not based on doing new things. *What I think is important for us to remember in the practice of science, is that we are a force of nature.* By discovering principles about how the universe works, and then applying them to cause *new* things to come about, we act as a force of nature! The mission of society lies in fostering new developments in that way and applying them, and *allowing* people to participate in that pursuit, whether directly as scientists or, as in the Apollo program, as a whole country, orienting the economy around a commitment to achieving something that led to results that were dramatic for all of mankind.

In reaching these higher levels, going from the world of the Stone Age, to the Bronze Age and the Iron Age, to the Age of the Steam Engine, to the Age of Chemistry—and these days we have a pretty good understanding of chemistry—we are able to create new materials; we're able to create new resources. We create resources! Uranium is a rock. One of its main uses before nuclear power was discovered, was to tint glass so that it wouldn't look purple. Now, it makes tremendous amounts of power.

The potential that we have in achieving a greater understanding of the nuclear world, and in having a mastery over the nucleus like the mastery we have to a pretty good degree over chemistry, will open up for us not just a dramatic amount of power, not just a *dramatic* transformation in our relationship to resources. Consider the use of resources. When we mine ores from the ground, they are rarely in forms that are directly useful to us. When we mine metals, they are basically rust. Iron ore is iron oxide. We have to remove that oxygen; we have to separate it; we have to turn it back into a metal. In doing that, we currently use chemistry. We introduce carbon to suck out the oxygen.

With a fusion torch, with which we are ionizing the atoms themselves and breaking them apart that way, you transform your relationship to materials *fundamentally*, by which you could—although it might not be effective or reasonable—simply mine dirt. Pass dirt through, separate out the different atoms that make it up. Our relationship to the material world will be transformed; our relationship to the Solar System will be transformed. With a mastery of nuclear rocketry, you could go to Mars and back in a week, as opposed to taking months and months and months, as today.

These are not things that we know how to do right now. They are things that we're getting closer towards.

Fusion research, in particular, has been *so underfunded* over the past decades, that it *has* to represent an intention *not* to make that breakthrough.

Zeus and Prometheus

Why anyone would want to do that? Why is there opposition, for example, to the Land-Bridge? That's maybe not so hard to gauge. We have the Project for the New American Century and the idea that "American military supremacy must remain unchallenged." We've got the Wall Street/City of London control over finance, threatened by a different turn in the economy. Why would a scientific breakthrough *itself* be opposed?

I will finish with an example of that, the Greek story of Prometheus. People are probably familiar with it. Prometheus saved mankind from being completely eliminated by Zeus, the king of the gods. Beyond that, Prometheus overturned one of Zeus's edicts. Zeus, he needed a therapist; he needed something to do with himself. Zeus, the King of Olympus, said that fire was only for him; it was not for the use of mortals. His identity lay in his superiority to them. If human beings developed, what would his identity be anymore? So, he said, "Forget it! It's forbidden!"

Prometheus, another one of the gods, took fire from Zeus and gave it to mankind. For this Zeus punished him, chained him to a rock. An eagle ate out his liver every day. He underwent torment. But, as the story goes, he gave mankind fire, poetry, astronomy, an understanding of the calendar for agriculture, the use of animals to do our tasks for us, medicine, number. He made us human.

That basis of our humanity, that fire in its various forms, that discovery of new sources of power through new understanding of the universe around us, that ability to transform who we are, and in so doing to really be ourselves in a scientifically cultural way—well, that is what makes us human. It is also under attack. We see that today, with the attack on the provision of power, as we heard in the message to the conference from Dr. Kelvin Kemm of South Africa, on the disgusting idea promoted by some visitors, saying, "Oh, Africans don't really need power; it's not their culture."

Poverty Is Intentional

People are people. The idea of "appropriate technologies" is completely reprehensible. But it exists today: preventing power from reaching people, preventing the development of the economy, using wars and conflict to prevent development, to break up the potential for the Silk Road, for example. As Sen. Dick Black went through, the instability in Syria is being deliberately promoted by the policies of the U.S. government—what's the point? What is the point of creating chaos?

In a sense, the fight over developing a scientific culture for the nation, the fight over developing a purpose for the nation, for society, for cooperation among nations, it stands up against some very major enemies. In promoting those principles you start to find out about those enemies. But in doing this, we always develop higher steps. We've never been done! We never will be. Our current resource base is a stepping stone to the future.

Imagine, before the introduction of the steam engine, if we had said, "We've got to save our wood resources." Wood was a very limited resource in the 1600s and earlier. What saved the wood, what saved the forests? Coal! Right! Coal, yes, it's limited, but we are certainly a fair way off from reaching its limit. But we have to use these resources that we currently have, towards achieving the *next higher* levels. For us today that would mean a major emphasis on fusion, on nuclear research—as nuclear research—to develop a mastery over that domain of nature that we don't currently have. It will provide us power; it will provide us transportation potentials, the ability to move through the Solar System and have a better control over it, to defend ourselves from asteroids; and it will transform our resource base and our relationship to raw materials.

There is no reason for poverty to exist *anywhere* in the world right now! The fact that it does, is a result of a political intention for it to exist. We certainly know how to grow food, we know how to provide power. But we shouldn't limit ourselves to the alleviation and elimination of poverty.

Where we *ought* to be, is so far ahead of where we are right now, that it is stunning. By creating cultural institutions in a society by which we are oriented towards developing to those higher levels, we provide people, each other, ourselves, an opportunity to live a life that we can look back on and say that the future will have judged it to have been necessary.

Individual Human Creativity Is the Key to Mankind's Future

Dennis Speed: The first thing I'd like to do is go to Lyn, since we haven't heard him live, and he's been listening the entire time.

Question: Good afternoon, Mr. LaRouche. I'm from Old Town, Maine, and I've been following you for decades. I'm glad you're still here with us. God bless you. I'm 65 years old, but when I was going to school in 1971 in Wichita State University, a lot of things were happening in education, and that was the beginning of where we started studying the future. Our textbook in that class about future change was about the dynamics of change. And keep in mind that 20-year-olds in that class were told that in 20 years' time, we were going to have 4-day work weeks, gerontology work as a job creator, leisure activities—people should major in those, so that when people get older … Pollution problems were going to be solved; everything was going to be great. Twenty years later, I'm in a class at Bangor at the University of Maine, and I heard the same thing. Well, now I'm 40 years older, and I'm not 20 years old anymore and naive. Greed and corruption stops it every time, and when we're talking about greed and corruption with all of this—space and whatever—it comes down to the petro-dollar Ponzi scheme scam that has been foisted on this world and everybody who takes part in that. People think oil is just fuel; it's textiles, it's pesticides, herbicides, pharmaceuticals, it's everything. Everybody who's making money off of that system wants it to continue, especially the ones at the top. All this fighting that's going on, the gas lines they wanted to go across Syria; blow Syria up. The Libya, the gold dinar—attack the corruption of the Federal Reserve petro-dollar Ponzi scheme scam. The central banks are private banks; people don't realize that, and we don't talk about it.

LaRouche: Yes, first of all, on this whole problem that he was presenting in the course of his blast—these considerations are really irrelevant. That is, the types of considerations that he has defined are absolutely irrelevant. They are based on an assumption which is a false assumption about the nature of mankind. Actually, mankind is a unique specimen, unlike any other known living creature. Only the human mind can create a new physical system, and the physical system is to be determined by the action of the mental system. That is the way science actually works. There are other interpretations, but they are mistaken. It is the human mind, and the human mind alone, that is capable of generating a new physical state in the practice of the Solar System or any other such system. Therefore, the idea of trying to make deductions from phenomena is a mistake. There are relationships of phenomena to these kinds of things, but they are understood only in terms of their being an effect; not as being a cause.

Question: I've been a full-time member for five years. Based on what the organization has accomplished in terms of bringing people together in different parts of the world, bringing governments together—there was mention of the LaRouche Youth Movement, which to my knowledge was started in the year 2000. We've obviously observed that we're not getting younger, and the LaRouche Youth Movement has gotten older, but there's always a new generation. There's always a new set of younger people. The idea of who will be the next LaRouche Youth Movement generation, or whatever metamorphosis that takes; if you could say something about that—with the idea that although we're organizing people, it's as important to see the people we're organizing as organizers. Rather than us organizing them, we are a tool, we're a resource that they can come to, to help them organize in the schools, etc. So, if you could say something on that.

LaRouche: It's wrong. There are aspects to that thing that are relevant, but the principle that you present is wrong. The character of the humanity of mankind is that the human individual, who has a voluntary creative power, in order to understand processes, is the individual, who actually *efficiently* defines the destiny of the human species, not just in one person, but in terms of the practice of mankind among persons. The usual interpretation of cause and effect in human behavior is wrong; it is the human mind's creative powers, and the human mind has a very specific kind of creative power. The creative powers of mankind are the source of the discovery of the principles of discovery, in themselves. Otherwise, no; it doesn't work. You get all kinds of recipes, all kinds of stories, but none of them really work when you go down and test the matter in detail.

Scientific Truth & the Human Mind

Question: I'd just like to bring up the subject of global warming and climate change. I wonder if you, Mr. LaRouche, would agree that fossil fuels are comparatively a very primitive form of energy generation, and that as the population of the Earth increases, it's hardly better than burning wood. We will simply not be able to sustain an advancing scientific civilization based on burning fossil fuels. I think maybe you might agree with that, and that instead we have to look at the energy flux density and move on to something more advanced, such as nuclear fission, fusion, etc. Pollution really is a big problem. They are using coal fuels over in Beijing, and the smog is so horrible people can hardly live. So, we do need to move on to something more advanced. But my other question is, can we avoid conflating that with this bizarre theory of global warming? In other words, even if global warming is false—which I believe it is—nevertheless, don't we need to progress to higher forms of

creative commons/Paul Wiesinger

"The human mind alone is capable of generating a new physical state in the practice of the Solar system, or any other such system." Johannes Kepler, who lived 400 years ago, discovered the Solar system. Here, a statue of Kepler in Linz, Germany.

energy generation?

LaRouche: No, that's not the way it works. Take the case of human behavior, first of all, and that simplifies what the issues are, possibly. First of all, all creativity of mankind is generated from the primary source of the creative powers of the human individual, not from some external source. See, that's what the difference is; what we call creativity in human behavior is the basis for the idea of what the principle of the human mind is. The human mind is driven by a *noetic* power; that is, a creative power which is independent of the individual per se—but which some individuals are capable of discovering and using to develop new things.

For example, Einstein. Now, Einstein is the only man who has succeeded so far in the past one hundred years in really understanding what is the basis of human behavior. Einstein was unique in this respect. In the recent one hundred years it has become obvious that he was right, and the others were wrong. You see, the way society is organized, mankind is organized by mankind's own actions; it is mankind's generated actions that create the failures or successes of human behavior. It is not something which you accept and experience by something that flew by you. Very few people understand this; most people are wrong. They don't understand how the human mind works. The human mind is a creative process which is unique, and it is the human mind's insight into principles, the discoveries of principles by the human mind, which creates the progress of mankind.

Speed: Very good. That's what I like to see; a man who's been completely confused by the right answer. We have another question over here.

Question: Mr. LaRouche, I come from Queens. My question is, what is the future of magnetic energy?

LaRouche: This is not the way to look at it. Look at everything that mankind does, accomplishes—everything that mankind as a species does, which no animal does. See, no animal can replicate the role of the human mind; no animal can do that if the animal is functional. In fact, all of the greatest creative forces in the history of mankind are governed by those principles. But the idea that you're getting a practical approach to solutions is a mistake. For example, the other kind works; it bounces. You have people who are, intrinsically, themselves creative people; they discover principles. They discover the experience of a principle, which may be their own achievement. They will become more excited about what they have discovered; they will then turn around and try to lead an audience to recognize what they have discovered as a creative principle. Now it's the people who think creatively, successfully, who actually make everything good about the human species; the others tend to be not so good.

Question: Hi, Lyn. This is Ian Brinkley, from Boston. I was thinking about how you've been responding to some of the questions here this afternoon, and it made me think of a particular problem which everybody who tries to engage in effective political organizing runs into—which is a certain kind of fear and anxiety which blocks the intention to convey a truthful idea when you see that you're encountering an individual or a group of people who don't understand something which they really need to understand.

LaRouche: Most people have that problem; and when you want to find out where the solution comes from, you have to look at the one case which is the most brilliant case of all: Einstein. Every physicist except Einstein was wrong on the crucial issues, and only recently have people begun to admit that Einstein was right on the question of gravity. So therefore, what you are talking about is a principle of gravity, and it's a principle of gravity whose characteristic is that it's peculiar to mankind. Einstein made discoveries which changed the course of the human species and changed the course of history. His mind did it. It is the human mind, when it is capable, which generates all of the great achievements of humanity—and it's often a minority of the human species which has the power to do that.

Question: Hello, Lyndon. We all know that there's a strong anti-growth movement, and they're scared that if we use up all our material, we will gradually die.

Ferdinand Schmutzer

"Einstein is the only man who has succeeded in the past one hundred years in really understanding what is the basis of human behavior." The others were wrong. Here, Einstein in a 1921 lecture.

Jason Ross gave us a great presentation on how our creativity can actually create new resources, like before nuclear power was not readily available. We discovered that. But this anti-growth movement will tell us, "Well, maybe our creativity will fail at one point. Is there a limit to our creativity? Is there one point where we will not be able to discover new things to replace our new technologies?" To that, I usually answer, "I prefer to believe that we will continue to discover, and I prefer not abandoning [our path]." I wanted to know what would you say? Do you have a better answer to that?

LaRouche: I would say the point is, the truth of the matter is collectively, individually, all useful developments—expressions of the human mind—are peculiar to the human mind. Anything that's valid belongs to that category of human mind. Now what happens is that this is not a perfect process, because you have a lot of people who make a lot of mistakes. Therefore, the answer is, the *effective result, the competent result* of

Jason Ross: LaRouche has emphasized the role of Bertrand Russell in the shift in science away from discovering totally new things. Here, Russell taking to the streets in protest in London in 1961.

put aside. Bertrand Russell had said in the 1890s, implicitly, that space couldn't possibly be curved, and that properties of matter couldn't be any different when you get into the very small. In the 1890s he said that the big discoveries of the 1900s would never happen; he said that there couldn't be a quantum, and that there couldn't be relativity.

So, in terms of the example of Einstein as having made a major discovery that overthrew what existed before, that didn't add to it, but *overthrew* what had currently existed—I think what he did as a personality was very important for thinking through what should science be.

Kesha Rogers: I think what is important to think about in this discussion that we're having right now is that we are not dealing with a practical political debate. It's not about up and down votes, and opinions, and whether or not you agree or disagree on a political view. You have to understand that this conference, and this panel in particular, is so important. There are very dividing issues on this panel, because Mr. LaRouche had something much more fundamental on these questions. This is a human debate! I just think about the fact that you take Krafft Ehricke—and I mentioned him earlier—he had a very profound concept of this idea of a closed world system versus an open world system. Right now we're still debating and living in a closed world system that cannot achieve the type of creative goals and breakthroughs which are necessary for mankind to foster its true creative potential. That's what you have to get at. So if you don't think your questions are being answered, it's because you are still stuck in that closed system, and you have to get out of it!

When I called for a space—and I hope to accomplish this—an international space panel, I wanted to take up this very fight, this very question that doesn't exist in our political arena right now! I ask the scientists, where are the politicians? They are not responding to real science; that's why I'm up here. That's why Mr. LaRouche and I are collaborating and working on this fight.

Mr. LaRouche is bringing up the genius of Einstein, and he more recently talked about the creative genius of

the human mind's work is to inspire a creativity which can be generated *only* by the human individual mind.

Discovering New Principles

Speed: Let me just take a moment and ask if there's anyone from the panel who has anything that they want to add or say.

Jason Ross: I can say something. One specific thing about whether we're going to finish discovering things or not: I think that this goes to a theme that Mr. LaRouche has been bringing up a lot over the past couple of years, which is the approach of Bertrand Russell, and the 1900 shift in science; where, away from discovering totally new things, the practice of science increasingly became, at least officially, put in terms of "Can you derive your new thought in terms of what we already know?" What Russell tried to do in mathematics, to turn mathematics into logic, got also applied to science in general. And the opportunity to say, "Hey, we just don't know everything yet; there is more to know," got

Below is a drawing by Leonardo da Vinci of a winch designed by the scientific genius, Filippo Brunelleschi, to construct the unprecedentedly large dome of Santa Maria del Fiore *cathedral in Florence, Italy. It still dominates the city.*

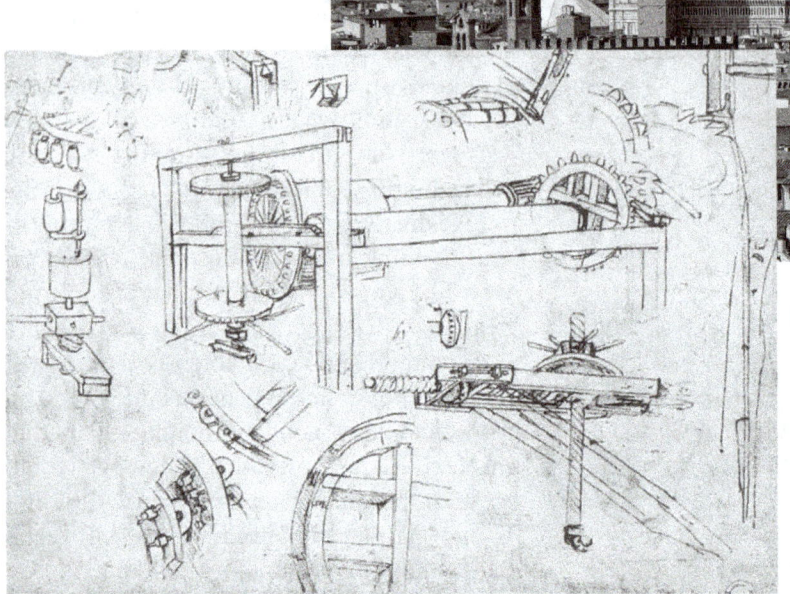

settled! We're getting new data *every day* about climate! We're learning things, we're learning relationships that we didn't know, and you need to *look at the data*. And that's one of the things that NASA's been pretty helpful in, in provided the data. It's the people who are *interpreting it*, and saying that there are no questions left to ask, that are on the wrong side of that issue.

So, keep your minds open, keep your target toward Mars.

Improving Your Way of Thinking

Question: I feel very honored to be here. I'm from Brooklyn. Something that I do want to say, that's always stuck very close to me, was, an instructor once said to me, while studying Buddhism, "to a beginner, there are many possibilities, but to an expert there are few."

Now I'm a beginner, and I'd like to keep a beginner's mind. I know nothing, but something I did come to understand from NASA's data, is that there is space junk. For the past 60 years, we have been throwing manmade junk into space. Is there a way to pick up where we left off and make use of and harness this space junk?

LaRouche: Science. Actual, efficient science! You may not be able to get a perfect correction of what the scientific principle is, but you can get closer and closer to it by experiencing your own errors in judgment.

The point is, *nonetheless*, that it is the *human individual mind* which is the only competent authority for

Brunelleschi, and I'd like for him to expound on that a little bit more. When we are talking about the process of creating these new cities, beautiful cities, creating a commitment to space, I think that's the example we have to use. Mr. LaRouche is talking about fostering a conception which most people don't think of; most people don't think of themselves as having genius, being geniuses, creating genius, having your children become geniuses. You can't do that in this society! It doesn't foster it. We have to do that here, today.

Tom Wysmuller: I could piggyback on something Jason talked about. He talked about Bertrand Russell saying that basically most of the science is behind us. When Einstein applied for a job at the patent office, and he worked as a patent clerk for a while, his boss told him, "there's no future here, because everything that's going to be invented already has." [laughter] So—that's the truth.

Now, these days, you're hearing a lot of stuff on the climate, and I want to address one of the questioners, that "the science is settled"! Well, guess what? It's *not* solving these problems. Now, some people are not as efficient in making these discoveries or developments, but nonetheless, the human being is *not* an animal. And the usual interpretation of human behavior is based on the presumption that mankind is an animal. That is when the mistakes are made.

Question: I completely agree with Lyndon LaRouche about the human mind, but for the same reason, I don't understand why such names as Tesla, for example—who is at least, maybe in my eyes, at the same level as Einstein—the great inventor of free energy. Nobody spoke about numerous free energies, carry energy; we never hear about it. The latest has to do with cold fusion; it's a major breakthrough, but nobody mentioned it. And I don't know why, because, although it's not very widely publicized, it's accessible. The majority of these guys—same destiny....

Speed: Excuse me. I think we're going to have to have your question repeated so we can all understand it.

Sare: He is asking about many inventions that have been made but have not been made available because there's a kind of Gestapo that prevents them from being allowed to be known.

Question: [follow-up] And among them are Tesla's inventions...

LaRouche: This is not a proper question. However, there are cases where the individual who's trying to follow something may not be able to make the efficient connection between the two facts of relationship.

But all creativity of mankind, that is of mankind as a social process, is based on a principle which is *unique to the human individual mind*. Now some people don't have an adequate development of the human mind, but if they are educated properly they can. The case of Einstein is clear. Einstein—as you know, an entire century has passed—Einstein has proven that on the basis of *his way of thinking*, not on the basis of some design, but on the basis of his way of thinking, he has made a discovery which has upset everybody.

So the point is, you have to understand that the source of creative powers of the human individual lies within the human individual, *not* within that nature.

Question: Mr. LaRouche, I was really overwhelmed by the Egyptian Consul who spoke in the morning panel, Mr. Farouk, and the way that Egypt handled getting into the Land-Bridge. Why can't we do that as

NASA

Kesha Rogers: Krafft Ehricke had a profound concept of an open world system. Here Ehricke demonstrates the plan for the interior of a space station.

Americans? Start our *own* fund, instead of waiting for the United States to turn around and say, "let's get on board"? Why can't we do this like Egypt did in financing the New Suez Canal, and tell the United States government to let us just take it on ourselves?

LaRouche: Well, you know the problem is, most of the members of the establishment in the United States today are crooks. They have strong opinions! And they believe in those opinions, or they pretend to believe in those opinions. And they do it, and they're scattered all over the place.

So you will need something a little bit better than that. You've got to understand one thing: The question is the mind of a scientist, specifically a scientist—or an especially good scientist, is his or her opinion, is it or is it not the source of the discovery of a principle which is otherwise *not* discovered? That's the issue.

Now, some people are better at that business and others are less good at that principle, but that is the principle. The entirety of mankind's success, as mankind, depends upon the creative powers, specific to some specific individual human beings—or else they're wrong! That's your alternative.

The medicine that is presented, is it correct or is it not? All the important things in science, all the important things in human individual knowledge, depend upon the validity of these kinds of discoveries. Without

CNTV

An international space panel does not exist in our political system right now, said Kesha Rogers. That is why it is so important to have the idea of creating geniuses. Our society is not doing that now.

that, maybe we will get accidentally lucky or something—that does happen; but the question is, when it comes to an actual principle, the creative principle, an efficiently creative principle is actually generated *uniquely* by the mind of a human individual. Now that individual may make mistakes, but the question of that individual's ability to make a discovery of that type, is what's crucial. And some people are good at it; some of them are not perfect at it. But the whole basis of the human process of human progress depends upon that principle. Otherwise, you've got nothing but animals!

Question: We have many enemies to genius, and you've come up against your share in your lifetime, so I guess this is more of a social science question in terms of, do you have any insight or a principle we might use to overcome this fear-based life that we were brought up in? I mean, where we've seen genius thwarted time again. We're here to bring something home where we can begin to instigate change. Any insights on that?

LaRouche: The only insight is, that the educational system of the United States is lousy. It could be improved!

Question: Mr. LaRouche, I totally agree with your creative moment and the individual. What is your position on synchronization of individual creative effort in terms of a mastermind community?

LaRouche: Oh, the problem is what happens is,

often we'll find that we don't know which end starts first sometimes. You sometimes get a child who turns out to be a genius, and that's a discovery. And then you find somebody who is supposedly a leading scientist who's a bum! So therefore, you have to understand that there are categories that you have to learn to be familiar with, in order to discern which person is probably likely right, or at least right to have an opinion.

The important thing: It's very important for all mankind to have access to human minds which are able to deliver, maybe not just from the start, but from somewhere in the process; who are able to actually understand something which is tantamount to an original, human principled discovery. That is what the whole thing is based upon. That's what every scientist does who's competent. The scientist will work and sweat and do all these kinds of things they do, in order to achieve something which is truth. And what they're trying to do is understand what the *truth* is of the matter.

And the whole system, of success of society and cultures as such, depends upon the ability of some people to make progress in discovery of human principles, absolute human principles, which are uniquely human. In other words, you cannot fake it; you cannot fake that. You cannot fake any kind of principle; you have to actually work, and fight your way through and find out what the truth is.

And Einstein, for example, is an ideal example of the kind of person in society who is capable of making those kinds of discovered things.

Question: Mr. LaRouche, I just want to address some things that this gentleman said and a couple other people said, in regard to what's going on out there in the world. There is a Gestapo-like organization, there are these banks, there is this stuff going on, and I disagree that we shouldn't be focusing on it, because I think it's possible, and not just possible, I think it's probable that the fire out there, that these people, these greedy, corrupt people will eat us alive, and burn us alive before we have the chance to go out to Mars and do these things. I think we need to really focus on that. So my question is, why would we *not* focus on that? Why would we not get down to the bottom of that and really address these criminals and these thugs?

LaRouche: Because the influence of the society's culture destroys the ability of the human being, the individual in many cases, to be responsible.

We should educate our people better and treat them more kindly.

Question: It's an honor to be here, and Mr. LaRouche, it's an honor to get a chance to ask you a question. I'm from Boston, Mass., and my question is that it seems like all around the world people are stuck in a comfort zone with things that they know work, and don't necessarily make the leap to newer technologies because of the lack of understanding and the lack of reliability being that it's new technology.

LaRouche: Your reference to a lazy mind, not coming up to a standard, is really the appropriate thing. People will say, "I feel more comfortable with what I think and the smell I exude, than I would with anything else." And therefore they like to smell themselves and feel that that smell is the good smell; and they will just walk away from everything with that, without considering what the proper smell of the animal should have been. And if it runs into a skunk, well, that's what the result is.

Fostering a New Renaissance

Speed: OK, let me ask, are there any summary remarks? Is there anybody from the panel, first of all, who wants to say anything, and then we'll go to Lyn.

Wysmuller: In answer to the young lady who said that when she was young, everything was possible, and then as she got older she found it wasn't. Well, the truth is, as you get wiser, you find out *again* that there is much more to find out in the universe than you've ever dreamed of.

We have a lot more to learn. We have a lot more to learn.

Speed: OK, Jason!

Ross: To be honest, I had a lot of specific thoughts on some of the specific questions. The only general conclusion is that it's just really important to develop a culture in this way.

This evening we're going have a panel on music, what we typically call "culture." Music, poetry. There's also a culture to science, and it's very easy to look at the fruits of science, or its effects, or what it does for you, and neglect the fact that there's a whole culture to the practice of science: How did a discovery get made? What were the people like who figured things out? How did they think?

And I think that there is as much—no, I won't compare—there's a great deal of beauty and insight that we can gather from that, just like we do with typical "culture." We need to have both of them, culturally, living in us.

Speed: Kesha?

Rogers: Well, I think I will end by saying that most of you came here today because you know that our society is in grave danger, and we're facing a grave threat to our existence as human beings, and you want to do something about it. I think if you take the discussion that we've had here today, and will continue to have— this idea of fostering a Renaissance for mankind—what is the requirement of mind, to truly bring that about? As we look at what is necessary to inspire beauty in our society, we have to actually rid ourselves of this—as Jason said—of this culture of degeneracy, of ugliness. Mr. LaRouche brings up Einstein—Einstein knew that the fostering of his creative mind also required participation in the beauty of great art, of great Classical music.

The way that you dumb down a society is to take away that potential for what makes us human, what makes us beautiful. That's what you should take from this conference. Be inspired to go out there and organize your communities. We have people represented here, of all different backgrounds, that in other countries, wouldn't be sitting together at all! We have a responsibility, here in the United States, to foster something that is what the United States was actually organized and created around in the first place—what our Founding Fathers had intended.

It's up to you! What about the United States? What are we going to do? How are we going to make the United States represent the greatness of who we are?

And so the United States has to join in this new mission, as I said, in fostering this new Renaissance, and this has to be taken as something real in all of our minds.

Speed: Lyn do you have any final remarks?

LaRouche: Just that I've learned a little bit from what people have as opinions, again from this experience here, which is highly variegated, of course, in terms of the composition of the whole. But some people get really fretful about protecting their something-or-other, and that is a little bit problematic at times. But I think it will clear its way out.

Land-Bridge Implementation

China-Pakistan Economic Corridor: The Challenges

by Ramtanu Maitra

In 2013, China and Pakistan signed a landmark agreement enabling China to build a corridor linking Kashgar in Western China's Xinjiang province to Pakistan's port on the Arabian Sea at Gwadar, called the China-Pakistan Economic Corridor (CPEC). This is the third article on the CPEC in consecutive issues of EIR.

April 11—An ambitious project such as the CPEC—which links China and Pakistan by traversing thousands of kilometers of deserts and mountains to reach the sea—is expected to face many challenges. Some are related to construction and maintenance engineering and the adequacy of preparations to participate in such a large project while carrying on with mundane but challenging daily activities. Some other challenges, however, are related to geopolitical complexities and ensuring security throughout the length and breadth of the project. All those residing in the region and participating in the CPEC project to bring it to life, will experience a kind of change that has escaped them for many decades.

Engineering and Maintenance Challenges

The first challenge is to keep the 1,300 km Karakoram Highway (KKH) functional throughout the year. The highway connects China and Pakistan across the Karakoram mountain range through the Khunjerab Pass at an elevation of 15,397 feet and took almost 27 years to construct. The transport corridor is vulnerable to landslides and voluminous snowfall during the winter—892 Pakistani and Chinese workers lost their lives while building the highway. In January 2010, the Karakoram Highway was submerged near the Khunjerab Pass due to a severe landslide in the Hunza valley that resulted in the formation of an artificial lake 30 kilometers long. Large sections of the KKH were submerged, causing a major disruption of traffic between China and Pakistan. It took five years to get the road

The Moon over part of the Karakoram Range as seen from Pakistan.

connected by land once again, making unnecessary a boat journey across the lake requiring an hour or more.

China realized that the highway will remain vulnerable in that area because of the geological instability and bare mountains carrying large and loose rocks. It solved the problem by tunneling through the mountain, forsaking the old, "romantic" Silk Road. It took three years and $275 million to complete the tunnel, an engineering miracle. Nonetheless, avalanches, heavy snow-

de:Benutzer:Grag/CC BY-SA 3.0

The Karakoram Highway. It links Pakistan to the ancient Silk Road city of Kashgar in Xinjiang province, China. The China-Pakistan border is at the three-mile-high Khunjerab Pass.

falls, and landslides will continue to be hazards and threaten certain sections of the road during the winter and rainy season, disrupting the flow of traffic. The area is also prone to floods.

Security

One of the challenges that Pakistan faces is that the western route of the economic corridor, leading directly to Gwadar Port, runs through a vast landmass where insecurity prevails. Pakistani officials point out that hostile forces, mostly based in the province of Balochistan, are openly against the construction of the CPEC and sabotage efforts to bring in foreign investments and integrate Balochistan with the rest of Pakistan. Balochistan has remained volatile since the founding of Pakistan in 1947, and some of its people have remained steadfast in seeking separation from Pakistan. The decades-long instability in Afghanistan that bor-

ders Balochistan on the west, and the consequent growth of terrorism, have contributed to the insecurity.

During the construction stage, this insecurity poses a threat to the Chinese workers and technicians on the project. The government of Pakistan in Islamabad has asked Beijing to put in place procedures to maximize security, including provision for security officials to have prior knowledge of the movement of Chinese personnel in the construction area. Pakistan has also established a Special Security Division of nine composite infantry battalions (9,000 personnel) and six civilian armed forces wings (6,000 personnel) to be headed by a serving major general of the Pakistan Army.

Islamabad has also set up the Gwadar Security Task Force under the command of a serving brigadier of the Pakistan Army to enhance protection and security in the Gwadar region, also located in Balochistan province. This was necessary because China had shelved several Gwadar-related projects a few years ago, after three Chinese engineers were killed by the insurgents.

Another security challenge is the semi-autonomous Federally Administered Tribal Areas (FATA) in Pakistan's northwest, bordering Afghanistan on one side and the province of Khyber-Pakhtoonkhwa on the other. The CPEC's western route will pass through Khyber-Pakhtoonkhwa, which shares the insecurity of the FATA, before it enters Balochistan to the south. A number of terrorist groups function in this area, including Uighurs from China's western Xinjiang Province. The Chinese have been putting pressure on Pakistan to ruthlessly pursue all of these groups, in particular the Uighurs of the separatist, al-Qaeda-linked East Turkestan Islamic Movement (ETIM).

Motivated to see the project implemented, Pakistan is taking measures. Its success cannot be ascertained at present. In the post-construction period, security will continue to be a key element in the success of the CPEC.

If China is investing so heavily in Pakistan megaprojects, as one Pakistani analyst pointed out, it is Islamabad's responsibility to develop its capacity building and professional skills to meet the deadlines for the construction of roads, railways, and power stations. Failure to meet deadlines will have a negative impact on the CPEC, and Beijing might then seek other options to obtain an outlet to the Arabian Sea, via Iran.

Geopolitical Conundrum

The CPEC enters Pakistan from China through the Gilgit-Baltistan region, which is part of the state of

Wikimedia Commons

One of the frequent, minor landslides along the Karakoram Highway. The monumental landslides, such as the one in January 2010, are the real threat.

problem. While Pakistan cannot make Gilgit-Baltistan a province, lest it contradict its long-standing claim to Jammu and Kashmir as a whole—and thereby sacrifice assured votes if the promised plebiscite should ever take place, to determine whether Jammu and Kashmir belongs to Pakistan or India—most local residents demand that Gilgit-Baltistan be made a province of Pakistan.

Despite Pakistan's caution in this respect, India-Pakistan relations still have an untoward impact on the CPEC project. Although India acknowledges the benefits it would derive from the CPEC if it were to be extended to connect with Indian markets, creating an overland route from India to the Central Asian markets, it has raised objections to the corridor's route through Gilgit-Baltistan, which India claims as part of the Indian state of Jammu and Kashmir. Gilgit-Baltistan has been under Pakistani control since the founding of Pakistan in 1947. India has objected to Pakistan's moves to assert ownership or consolidate control over what it considers Indian territory under Pakistani occupation.

Jammu and Kashmir, a state that remains disputed between Pakistan and India. Gilgit-Baltistan is located in the Pakistan-occupied part of the state, but instead of integrating the residents as citizens, Islamabad has accepted them into Pakistan only for administrative control. Pakistan is now in a quandary how to deal with this